# INVESTOR RELATIONS: THE COMPANY AND ITS OWNERS

# INVESTOR RELATIONS: THE COMPANY AND ITS OWNERS

AMERICAN MANAGEMENT ASSOCIATION
NEW YORK

Library of Congress catalog card number: 63-23297

This is No. 78 in the series of AMA Management Reports.

## CONTRIBUTORS

*Corliss D. Anderson*
*Robert R. Augsburger*
*Walter R. Boris*
*John E. Canfield*
*William E. Chatlos*
*John F. Childs*
*H. Peter Converse*
*Raymond J. Dodge*
*James A. Farmer*
*John A. Gearhart*
*J. Hervie Haufler*
*Matthew F. Kane*
*T. Howard Keelor*
*Ruddick C. Lawrence*
*Franklin Moore*
*William C. Norby*
*John K. Ottley III*
*Lowell E. Pettit*
*William L. Phyfe*
*Frederick N. Robinson*
*Stanley Sauerhaft*
*O. Glenn Saxon, Jr.*
*Frank B. Smith*
*Rudy L. Vincenti*
*Gale D. Wallace*

## EDITOR

*Jerome W. Blood*

# CONTENTS

COMPLETING THE TASK

# SECTION I

---

## *An Overall View*

*A company must be convinced of the value and importance of investor relations before it embarks on a detailed program. Following this, it would do well to put into some kind of perspective the great variety of activities and techniques involved in a total investor relations program.*

# THE IMPORTANCE OF INVESTOR RELATIONS •

LOWELL E. PETTIT

THE RAPID EXPANSION OF INVESTOR RELATIONS activities over the past ten years demonstrates management's increasing concern for the interests of share owners and investors generally. It takes only a glance at the material covered in the following chapters to see not only the scope and complexity of modern investor relations but also the breadth of fresh ideas and new techniques that are being applied as companies seek to strengthen this important segment of business operations.

In the rush to develop this long-neglected area of company relationships, it is sometimes easy to overlook the underlying philosophy and purpose and to focus on the immediate objective of some particular activity or program rather than the total, long-range goals. And so in the face of all these new approaches, techniques, and practices, it is well to take a look at the needs of the business and the responsibilities to the share owners on which a sound investor relations program must be based.

## BASIC RESPONSIBILITIES TO THE SHARE OWNERS

At the very core of this work and transcending all other considerations is the fact that we deal basically with the owners of the business. As owners they have a right to receive continuous, comprehensive reports of the responsibility for their investment which they have entrusted to the board of directors; they have a right to vote at the annual meeting fully informed

LOWELL E. PETTIT is Manager—Investor Relations Service, General Electric Company, New York, New York.

about the issues involved; and they have a right to expect ready marketability of their stock at a fair price.

To some extent, the owners' right to receive information is provided by law or regulation, or formal agreement; but mere conformity to such requirements is no longer acceptable to a growing majority of share owners. From the increasing penetration of the specialized financial analyst who represents a large holding, to the simple but earnest questions of the student with his first share of stock, the demands for more information are growing steadily. Management has little choice but to meet these demands with programs which will better communicate all the information about the business to which its owners are entitled.

Another fundamental right—which is too often overlooked or ignored—is the maintenance of the marketability of the stock at a fair price. For example, Graham and Dodd in their famous book on security analysis say: "It is fully as important to the stockholders that they be able to obtain a fair price for their shares as it is that the dividends, earnings, and assets be conserved or increased."* With the stock exchanges maintaining one of the few remaining free market auctions, prices are set minute by minute by the buyers and sellers. In the longer run, however, prices are strongly affected by those who refrain from buying and refrain from selling. Nearly all of these actual or potential buyers and sellers are influenced by what they know about a particular company and what they know about other competitive investment opportunities.

Therefore, marketability at a fair price requires a continuous effort to give as many of these people as possible as much factual information about the company as it is feasible to release. This not only reinforces the need for full communication with those who now own the company but adds to this audience the whole range of potential share owners—those who could own some of the company's stock even though they do not now do so—and the financial community as well.

These two fundamentals—full reporting and concern for a fair market price—constitute the minimum which must be met by any investor relations program. There is no doubt in most cases that they will sooner or later be enforced both by outside regulation and by the share owners themselves.

The New York Stock Exchange, for example, by means of listing agreements and promotional efforts, is continually working to bring about better, more comprehensive reporting to share owners. Some of the proposed

* Graham, Benjamin, and Dodd, David L., with the collaboration of Charles Tatham, Jr., *Security Analysis: Principles and Techniques,* McGraw-Hill Book Company, New York, 1951.

changes in Securities and Exchange Commission regulations arise from and are directed at instances of incomplete or misleading reporting of company information with its possible effect in creating unfair market prices.

Pressure on the company also comes from the share owners themselves who are becoming more active and articulate in pointing out what they consider to be shortcomings of the investor relations program. They want more complete, more factual, more understandable annual reports; and they want interim reports as well. They want full information and discussion of the issues in the proxy statement so their votes can be informed ones. Their growing attendance at annual meetings and their participation in the discussion show a desire to supplement the printed material with additional information obtained in person. And, of course, the share owner support, however small or misguided, that is attained by the self-appointed champions of so-called share owner rights may be a symptom of active demand for better investor relations.

The trend of the professional investors—banks, investment companies, insurance companies, and other financial institutions—is also in the direction of wanting better information. With their fast-growing holdings of common stocks, they must take an increasing interest in the affairs of the companies in which they have invested. Furthermore, the financial analysts who represent these institutions are becoming more professional and more specialized in their interests and assignments. As an analyst becomes more knowledgeable about the companies he follows, his needs for information grow in scope and sophistication.

Just as marketing leadership requires extra value in the products, so good investor relations today demands that a company must go beyond the minimum requirements. To do more than merely meet these basic responsibilities to the share owners means little additional cost to the company, and the rewards in share owner understanding and support are great.

### THE POTENTIAL POSSESSED BY SHARE OWNERS

The share owners are a great potential source of strength for the company—a resource largely untapped today—as ready suppliers of capital, as customers and ambassadors for the company's products or services, and as active and vocal supporters of efforts to achieve a better economic climate in which to operate. Predisposed toward the company and the private enterprise system, the share owners, with their financial stake and special interest in the business, are a willing audience for broadened programs developed in these directions. These potential sources of strength are important enough to be discussed briefly.

*As sources of capital.* With the huge amounts of capital required for expansion and modernization, business must look ever more carefully at the possible sources of this money. Retained earnings are commonly the source of a major portion of these funds. The continuous flow of retained earnings and the absence of direct cost often make them superior to other sources of capital. The very simplicity of raising money by this method obscures the fact that in the long run this can be done only because the share owners have confidence in the company and its management.

Of course, such confidence can only come from sound business performance. But time after time it has been demonstrated that good performance by itself will not build this confidence unless it is thoroughly reported. The bare operating results must be enhanced and fortified by telling the story factually, actively, and continuously through an effective communications program. At the same time, this situation sounds a warning for investor relations in that nothing can destroy this confidence faster than predictions and promises which cannot be fulfilled.

On those occasions when the company must obtain additional capital through the sale of securities, a sound investor relations program which has been carried out over the years may well prove its value in more concrete terms. The process of supplying company information to the share owners, financial analysts, and the financial community—if done honestly and willingly and effectively in the regular course of business—cannot help but establish an understanding of the company which will make it easier to obtain these funds when they are needed. And this result can be expected whether the securities are offered to the share owners or to new investors.

As a matter of fact, the advisory services, financial publications, brokerage firms, and others in the financial community represent a main communications channel to potential investors who must some day become investors in order to increase the body of share owners from whom the company must seek its ever larger future capital requirements. For a growing company, therefore, a broad and enlightened investor relations program can go a long way toward assuring an adequate supply of needed capital both now and in the future.

*As customers.* Expansion of the investor relations program in the direction of cultivating the share owners as customers and ambassadors for the company's products and services can assist the company's marketing efforts. It is generally believed—and in our own case, at least, definitely confirmed by survey findings—that share owners consciously favor their company's consumer products when they buy for their own use. Furthermore, many of them voluntarily make an effort to help by recommending these products to their friends and neighbors.

The story of new and improved products and services is a natural part of the company's reporting to its owners. To many share owners it is the most tangible part of this reporting and one which stimulates the greatest personal interest, particularly when it can be translated in terms of their own individual experiences. In fact, asking share owners what additional information they would like to have is almost certain to bring requests for more data about products. This is one case in which judicious additions to the basic investor relations program can actually result in increased sales and profits. However, it is important to be judicious because these people want and deserve to be treated as owners of the company and not mere candidates for a mailing list for direct mail advertising campaigns.

Naturally the greatest impact of these efforts will be in the area of consumer products and services, but the share owners can be helpful with other product lines as well. Producers of raw materials encourage their share owners to select the utensils, clothing, or furniture made from the company's product. Office equipment companies make use of the fact that many of their share owners are employed in positions where they can recommend the company's products to their employers. Where the product is more technical, some companies are asking their share owners to supply sales leads which are turned over to the regular sales force. Every day the share owners are in a position to help create an atmosphere in which the effectiveness of the sales and advertising efforts of the company in all of its lines of business can be multiplied.

*As allies.* Share owners tend to be prominent citizens in the community, influential in its affairs, active in its many organizations, and substantial contributors to its daily life. For these reasons, they generally can be articulate and influential proponents of the private enterprise system, as well as potentially active and vocal supporters of the company nationally and in the communities in which it operates. In the area of economic issues which affect the company, they are ready to listen and to help. More and more, in fact, they are beginning to ask how they can help and why they have seldom been asked to do so.

An investor relations program can readily be extended in this direction with results which are of value to the company. If they are well informed and made aware of their interests, share owners can:

1. Contribute to a fuller understanding of the private enterprise system —the role of profits; the need for investment; the effect of restrictions, overregulation, and high taxes—among their friends and neighbors.
2. Give personal evidence that companies large and small are owned by a broad cross section of the American people.

3. Spread understanding of the company and its role, its actions, and its policies in the whole economy and in the communities in which it operates.
4. Provide strong national or local support when called upon either as a group or as selected individuals to proposals for reasonable taxation, legislation, and regulatory policies; to the demand for adequate community services and the many other things which add up to a better climate in which to conduct the business.
5. Help mobilize community opinion and secure approval and understanding of the company's positions and actions in times of crisis.

The share owners' personal participation in our economic system means that they are living a course in economics. To help them understand it, to make them fully aware of their own interests, to stimulate them to become active supporters on economic issues and representatives among their friends and neighbors, takes little extra effort aside from the bare essentials of any investor relations program. But the payoff might well be the reinforcement that our private enterprise business system needs.

### BROADENING SHARE OWNERSHIP

One important objective of a modern investor relations program ought to be the broadening of share ownership in the company and in business generally. It is good for the individual to add an ownership dimension to his participation in the private enterprise system. It is good for the company to have a broader base of ownership from which to obtain the capital and the active interest and support it will need. It is good for the country to have more and more active individual capitalists interested in risk taking with the expectation of receiving a profit.

The primary responsibility for broadening the ownership of stock lies, of course, with the brokerage firms and the rest of the financial community. But every company can and, I think, should make some effort to spread knowledge and understanding of the benefits of share ownership and cooperate actively with other organizations working toward this goal. There are no immediate tangible returns from this effort, but the job needs to be done better and faster. Business can help because it has an outstanding story to tell.

### THE INCREASED SCOPE OF THE JOB

All of these considerations, therefore, whether arising from legal requirements, share owner demands, management desires, or the needs of our economic system, require that we have a more comprehensive program of communication between the company and its share owners. The audience as a whole is more than willing to listen and is favorably inclined toward the company. Factual information, presented discreetly and moderately, will fall on fertile ground.

Clearly, a program which embraces these objectives is quite different from those which are called *share owner relations* programs. As is so often the case when a careful examination is made, companies have found that the needs and the scope of this area of vital business relationships have become much wider than they used to be. And this is the main reason for the adoption of the term *investor relations:* it describes more adequately the field as we know it today.

Investor relations includes the old idea of maintaining relationships with the share owners of record just as the modern marketing function includes sales efforts. But it goes on from this to embrace relationships with potential share owners—individuals and institutions that could but do not own the company's stock or even any stock. It makes use of communications channels of all kinds and encourages financial intermediaries and organizations, statistical and advisory services, brokerage firms, and financial publications to help in the effort to reach a wider audience. It recognizes the wide variety of needs, background knowledge, and interests from the smallest individual share owner to the largest financial institution and tries to conduct programs which will be meaningful and satisfying to each. It makes use of its ready-made opportunities to advance the level of economic understanding and political sophistication and to gain growing recognition of share ownership as a vital contribution to our economic well-being and as a mutually rewarding experience. And within the company it tries to increase awareness, understanding, and knowledge of the importance of the share owners, their role in the company, and their interests and desires, so that the voice of the share owner can be properly heard amid the everyday clamor of customers, employees, suppliers, and government.

In many companies the increased scope and depth of the investor relations program have come about gradually and with little fanfare. A comprehensive program is built on the same basic elements and uses the same basic techniques that we knew in the past but expands their usefulness and modifies their content to serve the new objectives.

Publications such as annual reports, interim and post-meeting reports, proxy statements, and others are the basis of an investor relations program. But they are made much more interesting and informative not just for one type of share owner but for the whole range of people who comprise the share owner group. They present a more comprehensive story and therefore are useful to both share owners and non-share owners. Each publication has its own basic purpose as always, but it must be carefully developed and programed so that every theme will supplement all the others and thus gain the greatest total communication effectiveness.

Share owner relations are carried out through the annual meeting, proxy solicitation, correspondence, and other personal contacts and special events. But these must be given new meaning and made to function as integrated parts of the whole investor relations effort. The annual meeting, for example, handled as a real source of information and participation for those share owners who attend, makes possible a more interesting and informative report of the proceedings for the great majority who cannot attend. And in the process it becomes the basis for sound and constructive news coverage and interpretation to the public, as well as a unique and worthwhile opportunity for financial analysts to supplement their normal contacts with the company.

Relations with professional investors and particularly the financial analysts must also be carefully coordinated with the rest of the investor relations program. Efforts to make publications and other activities more informative for the mass of share owners can also make them more useful as sources of information for the financial analyst. This and the fact that they will provide him with new insights into management ability, character, and philosophy can reduce the time required in personal discussions with individual analysts. This coordination is increasingly necessary also to guard against the dangers of giving an analyst "inside" information—to make sure that the same question will always be given the same answer whether it comes from a financial analyst or any other share owner.

Research and analysis also play a vital role in a sound program of investor relations. It is necessary to obtain specific information about the share owners which will help determine the direction which investor relations efforts should take. Measurements of the readership and impact of publications and evaluations of the other activities can repay their cost by insuring effective use of the money that is spent by pointing out shortcomings and suggesting possible improvements. Analysis of internal and external data will provide additional clues to the success of the program and suggest ideas that can profitably be developed in future communications.

These four main elements—publications, share owner relations, professional investor relations, research and analysis—tend to exist in some form in most company organizations. To carry out a full investor relations program effectively requires that they be carefully integrated into a single plan.

A large diversified company may find it necessary to bring this work together into a function staffed by a number of individuals, or a company with fewer share owners and less diversified interests may not require the full time of even one individual. But in any case the best results will be attained when all of these activities are coordinated, each element playing its part supplemented and fortified by all the others and all aimed at the common goals and objectives of the total investor relations program.

* * *

Some writers—perhaps critical of business to begin with—profess to see in wide share ownership a breakdown in control of the business by its owners, leaving management to run the business unrestricted. They translate this into a need for the exercise of control by people separate from both management and share owners.

Among other things, this overlooks the fact that the share owners have hired management to run the business for them. And any company that considers the share owners as simply another group whose favorable opinion should be cultivated also overlooks this fact as well as the responsibilities that go along with it.

As owners of the company, the share owners are the basic source of authority and capital and therefore are entitled to full and factual reporting of management's performance. Beyond this, management needs to give the same careful consideration to investor relationships that has been accorded to the development of other basic relationships—with customers, employees, and suppliers, for example. In the long run, the full potentialities of the business can only be achieved when concern for these other groups, on whom the success of the business depends, is fully matched by concern for the interests of the present and future share owners, without whose capital the business could not exist and grow.

# A TOTAL INVESTOR RELATIONS PROGRAM •

MATTHEW F. KANE

THE COMPOSITION OF A TOTAL PROGRAM of shareholder relations will depend upon a number of variables within any given company, among which are the characteristics of the shareholder group, the nature and extent of the business, and the organization and policies of the company. Therefore, I have chosen to approach this subject by describing the program which Standard Oil Company (New Jersey) has developed over a period of years in order to carry out its shareholder relations policy and to accomplish the objectives that seem appropriate and desirable for the company and its owners. We do not mean to advance our program as a model for all, and we recognize that such a comprehensive program would be inappropriate for many other companies.

As background to our program, a brief description of the organization and scope of the business activities of Jersey Standard may be helpful. The company has been in existence for over 80 years. It is engaged in the petroleum and chemical business through its direct or indirect investment in some 200 affiliated companies operating in over 100 different countries throughout the world. Standard Oil Company (New Jersey) is the parent company in this large family of affiliated companies and does not engage in the operating functions of the business. It is managed by a board of directors, all of whom are employees of the company.

Jersey Standard is owned by over 700,000 shareholders of record and an estimated additional 150,000 shareholders whose stock is registered in nominee or broker names. Ninety-eight per cent of the shareholders reside in the United States, and the other 2 per cent are located in over 90 foreign countries. In common with many other companies, we have experi-

---

MATTHEW F. KANE is Manager, Shareholder Relations, Standard Oil Company (New Jersey), New York, New York.

enced a broadening in the basis of ownership, which was accelerated in the postwar period and resulted in a tripling of the number of shareholders during the last ten years.

An important factor which has a significant effect on our shareholder relations program is the long-standing policy of the Jersey board of directors toward its responsibilities to shareholders and its decision, taken many years ago and only recently endorsed again, to retain for itself the responsibility for shareholder relations. The board has adopted a statement of policy on shareholder relations which recognizes management's responsibilities to shareholders and acknowledges its obligation to inform them fully and promptly, to answer their questions, and to study carefully their suggestions and criticisms.

The Jersey board has established a Shareholder Relations Division in the corporate secretary's office to provide assistance to individual directors and officers in their relations with shareholders. The following responsibilities have been assigned to that division:

1. To develop and maintain channels of communication with institutional and individual shareholders.
2. To exercise general supervision over communications and coordination of the activities of other departments and affiliates of the company which involve relations with Jersey shareholders.
3. To assemble information about Jersey shareholders and keep abreast of the shareholder relations activities of other companies.
4. To exercise general supervision of the agents appointed by the board to handle registration and transfer of stock and the payment of dividends.
5. To handle all arrangements for annual and special meetings of shareholders.

A number of shareholder relations activities and programs have been adopted to carry out the board's policy and to discharge the responsibilities entailed. Since Jersey's shareholders may be divided into two general classifications, activities under the program are organized into: (1) those which deal primarily with individual shareholders and (2) those which are oriented toward the institutional shareholders.

In its fundamental approach, Jersey's relations with its individual and its institutional shareholders are the same. However, institutional investors tend to be more knowledgeable about the company and the industry, to seek more factual data, and to raise more perceptive questions. We would be doing no service for the elderly widow who owns 50 shares were we to deluge her with the amount of detailed and technical information that the oil analyst for a large metropolitan bank may need in order to do his job.

## RELATIONS WITH INDIVIDUAL SHAREHOLDERS

Jersey's individual shareholders, who represent about 90 per cent of the total shareholder group, include a variety of people in all walks of life, some of whom are also customers, suppliers, or employees. Their one common bond, so far as the company is concerned, is the interest they have shown in Jersey Standard by electing to invest their money in its stock. Since our total shareholder group is so sizable and widespread, regular communications with all of them must necessarily be through mass media. Therefore, our program provides for the regular distribution to all shareholders of the publications described below:

1. *The Lamp,* which is a 24-page magazine published four times a year. The purpose of *The Lamp* is to serve as an attractive medium through which information about the company may be communicated to shareholders and to other segments of the public. In order to attract a high readership, there has been extensive use of photographs and art work and there is variety in the style and content of the articles appearing in the magazine. Over the years, readership surveys have indicated that these efforts appear to have been successful. One of the features of *The Lamp* is a message from the chairman of the board to shareholders in which he comments on topics which merit the special attention of the shareholders.
2. Another publication which reaches the shareholders on a quarterly basis is a pamphlet entitled *Jersey Shareholders' Quarterly.* It is enclosed with the dividend checks and includes interim financial and operating data as well as other brief articles of interest regarding current activities of the company and its affiliates.
3. Once a year the management sends to all shareholders its proxy statement soliciting their support in the form of proxies for the annual meeting. Our proxy statement includes photographs and brief résumés of the business background of each of the nominees for director, with the thought that shareholders should have the opportunity to learn more about and evaluate the competence of the men for whom they are voting. Efforts have been made to design the proxy statement in an attractive manner so that it does not have the character of a purely legal document.
4. Together with the proxy statement, we mail the company's annual report. The report is periodically reviewed to insure that it continues to satisfy the major purpose of that publication—to report to the shareholders on the stewardship of the board and to present, within the limits of reasonable size, an interesting report on significant

developments and progress of the company during the year. Charts and photographs are used to supplement the printed text, and a letter from the chairman and one from the president preface the report.

5. For those shareholders who express an interest in receiving it, a printed summary report of the annual meeting is made available in booklet form. In preparing this booklet, an effort is made to capture the spirit of the meeting, and a dialogue rather than narrative style is followed. For many years we mailed the report of the meeting to the entire shareholder list. Several years ago after a test of the readership of all of our publications, we concluded that the interest in this publication was limited. Accordingly, we decided to offer a copy of the report to those who requested it by returning a card which is enclosed with one of our dividend checks. We have been getting about 12 per cent response to that offer.

A sampling of the opinion of individual shareholders regarding our publications is taken from time to time. Those surveys have been useful as a guide to the format and types of material which are included in our publications. They have also been helpful in providing us with other interesting data about shareholders' views. Because the program of publications is a rather costly one, it seems important to evaluate it periodically.

The tone of our publications is intended to convey to the individual shareholder our "open door" policy and to assure him he is welcome to contact the company whenever he feels moved to do so. On his part, the individual shareholder may be motivated to write the company because he feels we are responsive to comments or suggestions. In fact, many have indicated in their correspondence with us that our publications have prompted them to write. Other communications from shareholders stem from matters pertaining to their stock accounts or are stimulated by information about the company or the oil industry which may be carried in the public press, on radio, or on television. Many comments also reach our office from shareholders regarding service rendered by dealers who distribute the products of our affiliates, and they often provide an opportunity for improvement in customer relationships. In all, some 15,000 to 20,000 individual shareholder contacts per year are handled through the company's offices.

Because we value the opportunity which an individual contact affords to make a favorable impression on the individual shareholder, all such contacts are channeled through our Shareholder Relations Division to insure that a prompt, courteous, and complete reply is made to each such communication. For the most part, shareholder communications reach the company in the form of letters, and replies to such letters are sent out over the signature of an officer of the company. Occasionally a telephone call or even a visit is the avenue of contact for a shareholder, and competent staff people are available to talk with the shareholder and provide him with proper service.

Many shareholders make direct contacts with our transfer agents who handle a variety of communications regarding address changes, questions about dividend payments, and matters pertinent to the transfer of stock. Because the impression made on shareholders in their contacts with our agents will reflect on the company, we satisfy ourselves that the agents' handling of such communications is in line with our policy. For example, we supervise our agents' use of printed forms to see that such communications are clear and not confusing to the unsophisticated shareholder.

When a person becomes a Jersey shareholder, he receives a letter from the chairman of the board indicating that his investment in the company has been noticed and welcoming him to the Jersey family. In this letter, a new shareholder is advised of the publications he will receive and is offered an opportunity to obtain a credit card which will make it more convenient to support his investment by becoming a regular purchaser of the products of our affiliates.

Once a year, the annual meeting provides an occasion for the management to meet face to face with a large number of shareholders. Without going into details on the meeting, which will be covered by others in this book, I will merely comment that our management regards it as a good opportunity to obtain insights into areas of shareholder concern and has encouraged shareholders to attend and participate. An invitation to attend, in the form of a letter from the chairman, is included along with the proxy statement. Our meetings are held in places that are convenient to many shareholders, and we take pains to provide comfortable facilities for the meeting. In recent years we have rotated the meeting to various cities in different parts of the United States and have attracted a large attendance, ranging from 2,000 to 4,000 shareholders. All of these meetings have been active ones, with from 30 to 40 different shareholders arising to address the chair. A key factor in encouraging such shareholder participation, which in turn diminishes the likelihood of one or two shareholders dominating the entire meeting, has been the system provided for a shareholder to address the meeting. A number of portable microphones are available throughout the meeting hall and are carried directly to the shareholder who seeks recognition so that it is not necessary for him to leave his seat to address the chair. Moreover, a considerable effort has been made to develop a sound system which permits all in the hall to hear the comments of both the shareholders and management without strain. Although luncheons have been served in the past at our meetings, and from time to time exhibits and movies were shown, these are not necessarily permanent fixtures. Our primary interest is to attract a number of shareholders to exchange views with management during the course of the meeting.

### PROGRAMS FOR INSTITUTIONAL INVESTORS

The institutional investors represent a variety of banks, brokers, foundations, insurance and investment companies, mutual funds, and pension funds which in the aggregate hold about one-half of our company's stock, much of it in a fiduciary capacity. Because of their important holdings and growing interest in our company, we have developed special programs and arrangements to handle the contacts with them. About five years ago, it was decided to centralize contacts with institutional investors within the Shareholder Relations Division. Prior to that time, financial analysts, investment advisors, and others representing institutional investors approached the company through a variety of departmental contacts and were handled by a number of individuals without a coordinated approach. Upon the establishment of a central point of contact, all executives within the company were advised of this channel for communications, and over a period of time the financial analysts and other representatives of institutional investors have become acquainted with this system. The volume of those contacts has grown steadily and now occupies the full time of one executive. Because of his knowledge of the areas in which the institutional investor is interested, as well as his acquaintanceship with the people in the financial analysts' community, he can more efficiently handle the volume of inquiries than would be possible if the contacts were spread through a number of executives with other responsibilities. The individual who handles contacts with analysts must be well informed about many phases of the company's activities, and part of his time has to be devoted to keeping abreast of developments so that he can effectively communicate with the sophisticated and knowledgeable persons who regularly approach him with questions. He also keeps in close contact with other executives of the company and occasionally, when highly specialized questions are involved, arranges for the analysts to meet with the executives best qualified to discuss their particular interests.

As a matter of policy, no information is given to institutional investors that would not be given to any shareholder. Our general approach in discussions with the analysts as well as with individual shareholders is to put forth appropriate information in answer to questions and let the investor make his own evaluations and projections.

In addition to the individual contacts with financial analysts, there are a number of other activities which are aimed primarily at institutional investors.

1. A periodic program of informal luncheon meetings is held in various cities where substantial concentrations of institutional holdings exist. These meetings are limited to some 30 guests and attended by a small group of company executives, including the chairman or president and several other directors. The objective of these meetings is to establish a rapport between the top management of our company and the senior executives of institutions with large Jersey shareholdings and the financial advisors to other substantial shareholders. Through this program we have kept in contact with such investors in about ten different cities over a period of more than 15 years.
2. Tours of properties of company affiliates are arranged from time to time for analysts' groups. Although we have no set program, such tours are generally tied in with analysts' meetings and afford them an opportunity to view some of the operating functions and research functions.
3. From time to time invitations are received to speak before analysts' groups. These invitations are carefully considered, and in many cases they are accepted if other demands on the time of our executives permit. As a matter of policy, our company has decided that only members of top management should be the spokesmen at gatherings of this type, which necessarily limits the number available to speak.

In addition to the activities of the Jersey shareholder relations program as described, there are others which certain companies have found to be useful, such as shareholder interview programs and regional meetings. Any company would certainly want to look at all the techniques which have been tried in order to develop a comprehensive program to best suit its own needs.

* * *

In summary, we believe that Jersey Standard's program is a well-balanced one which provides appropriate service and information to all the shareholders and at the same time gives special attention to that important segment which requires more information about the company. It seems to serve the interests of all the shareholders, and it provides the management with a two-way avenue of communication which gives shareholders sufficient information about the company and, in turn, identifies areas of shareholder concern. Thus, the board of directors becomes aware of and is responsive to the reasonable wishes and views of the owners of the company.

# SECTION II

---

## *Share Owner Relations*

*The measures adopted by a company to communicate with the individual—as contrasted with the institutional—investor fall under the category of share owner relations. Some of these activities such as the annual meeting and proxy solicitation are regulated by law or formal agreement. Others such as regional meetings, programs of share owner correspondence, and mobilizing share owners for special projects are conducted by forward-looking companies seeking the maximum participation of share owners in company affairs.*

# A BALANCED PROGRAM IN SHARE OWNER RELATIONS •

H. PETER CONVERSE

MANAGEMENT HAS A DOUBLE responsibility to the share owners of the corporation: the first half is to manage the business effectively so as to produce the maximum profit possible for the owners, and the second is to see that share owners are aware of the corporation's progress and are satisfied that the business is being effectively managed.

Although there is some truth to the assumption that a good dividend (or a high stock price) is worth reams of share owner literature, performance and profits alone do not produce good share owner relations. This is because the modern, publicly listed corporation has little choice as to who its owners are, since its shares are bought and sold on the open market for reasons largely unknown to management. The measure of the satisfaction of the share owners depends on their expectations at the time they make their investment decisions to buy or hold the shares. However, what the owners expect may be far greater, or far less, than the actual potential of the corporation.

This characteristic of ownership—the remoteness of the owners from the managers—illustrates the close affinity of share owner relations with general public relations. This affinity is further demonstrated by the fact that the public's evaluation of the potential of the corporation has a direct effect on the value of the share owners' investment.

In effect, share owners and the public are on one side of a wide gulf and management on the other. Some bridges across this gulf exist in the form of share owner publications, corporate publicity, and particularly in the person of members of the financial community. Security analysts, for example, are playing an increasingly important role in

---

H. PETER CONVERSE is Manager, Investor Relations, Sperry Rand Corporation, New York, New York.

communicating the substance of what a corporation is to the investing public—a public composed of potential share owners as well as current share owners.

The primary objective of share owner relations, however, is more than just establishing communications links across this gulf; it is creating knowledgeable ownership—ownership which will support management's efforts to further the fortunes of the enterprise and ownership which will correctly appraise the operations of the business and its potential.

With this broad objective in mind, developing a balanced share owner relations program becomes a process of establishing specific objectives which are consistent with the individual needs of the particular company, selecting the appropriate program elements from the wealth of techniques and practices discussed in other chapters of this book, and establishing the organization to do the job.

## ORGANIZATION OF THE PROGRAM

A brief review of the major elements of a share owner relations program will probably indicate that much of the job is currently being done by various corporate officers or assistants, for the nature of share owner relations is such that it cuts across many staff functions. For instance, the president may be personally concerned with correspondence with share owners; the treasurer, or chief financial officer, probably has a deep interest in contacts with security analysts and other members of the financial community; the secretary or legal counsel may be concerned with proxy solicitation and the legal requirements of the annual meeting; and the format and content of such share owner publications as the annual and interim reports may be a public relations matter. This division of labor makes the task of establishing specific objectives more difficult and, simultaneously, more important.

Throughout industry there appears to be no consistency as to where the share owner relations function falls organizationally. Some companies have pulled the various facets together into one department, but the head of that department in some cases may report directly to the president, in other cases to the treasurer, the secretary, or the vice president for public relations. Other companies have operated successfully by dividing up the tasks, although this increases the difficulty of creating an integrated program with specific objectives. Determining the company's specific objectives in investor relations is of paramount importance; the selection of the elements of the program or who performs them is secondary.

## ESTABLISHING SPECIFIC OBJECTIVES

To establish specific objectives, answers to two key questions must be found: What sort of support does the company want from its share owners? What is the current attitude of share owners toward the company?

The answer to the first question is a matter of management judgment and will depend on such diverse elements as the product mix of the company or the condition of its balance sheet. For example, a company selling consumer products will recognize that share owners are potential customers and therefore will design programs with a greater emphasis on sales promotion. At the other extreme, a firm which is considering the adoption of equity financing at some future date will be particularly interested in seeing that share owners and potential share owners are exposed to adequate, accurate knowledge as to the company's operations so that its shares are fairly appraised.

The answer to the second question, concerning share owner attitude, requires an amount of research proportional to the degree of refinement desired in the answer. For example, an indication of the current attitude can be obtained from comments voiced by share owners at the annual meeting or expressed in letters from share owners. This, of course, is not a valid statistical measure, since the comments come from a very small percentage of share owners, but it at least indicates the subjects on which there are strong opinions. Another informal measure of opinion is feedback from security analysts and other members of the financial community.

A clue to the views of share owners can be gathered from census data obtainable from the transfer agent. An analysis of accounts by size of holdings and a study of the distribution of accounts and distribution of shares by type of holder can help initially shape the format and direction of investor relations efforts. A record of the age of the accounts—for example, how long a certain percentage of the share owners have held their shares—compared with the historical record of dividends and price ranges of the stock can indicate the relative satisfaction of the share owners. Such steps help lay the foundation for establishing specific objectives, but more formal research is of immeasurable value.

## APPRAISING PROGRAM ELEMENTS

In the determination of specific objectives, it is apparent that program elements desirable for one company may not be necessary for another. For example, detailed plans for the annual meeting will depend upon the other purposes which the individual corporation wishes the meeting to serve in addition to fulfilling the legal requirement to hold an annual meeting of share owners. The annual meeting can be used in a variety of ways:

1. It can be an effective method of two-way communication with individual share owners.
2. It can be a sales promotion vehicle for consumer products.
3. It can be a public platform to disseminate knowledge of present company progress or future potential.
4. It can be effectively "merchandised" through post-meeting reports so that its significance is extended to a larger segment of the share owner group than the relatively small percentage who attend.

The decision to add tours or exhibits or provide lunches for share owners depends upon how desirous management is to attract large numbers.

Although a well-attended annual meeting with added features can improve communications with stockholders and create institutional goodwill, this may have little effect on the percentage of eligible shares voted or how they are voted. A good vote is the result of effective proxy solicitation efforts, and these have little to do with increasing attendance.

In appraising program elements, there is always the matter of expense. Little argument is required to justify the costs of the basic and necessary work, but beyond that it becomes hard to measure the value that will accrue from extra efforts—particularly those in the intangible area often referred to as enhancing the corporate image. For instance, should the annual report be printed in four colors or in just one or two? It is a known fact that some stockholders are displeased if the company "wastes money on fancy reports." It is also a known fact that the report has to be attractive enough to entice busy individuals to open it, let alone read it.

There are many "extra efforts" beyond the basic reporting activities which can be undertaken. For instance, institutional advertising campaigns, welcome letters to new share owners, display programs, or regional share owner meetings are often desirable and in many cases can be important. However it is hardly ever possible to measure the value of such extra efforts in dollars and cents. Nevertheless, they contribute to the shaping of public and share owner opinion, which eventually has a very definite impact on corporate profitability.

* * *

Taking a broad view of share owner relations and balancing its objectives with other corporate objectives, we should remember that share owners, in addition to having a personal stake in the profitable success of the corporation, are everywhere. Knowledgeable share owners may be loyal customers, suppliers, or employees. Furthermore, a well-informed group of share owners and potential share owners in addition to directly supporting the company—by adequately appraising its securities, for example—can support it indirectly in their role as citizens.

Corporations cannot operate without profits; and fiscal irresponsibility on the part of government is as great a deterrent to profits as fiscal irresponsibility on the part of corporations would be. The great challenge is successfully to impress the public and its elected representatives with the importance of profits as the motivating force in the business system—a force that begins by allowing the investor who is financing the machinery of production a fair return on his investment. The millions of share owners in the nation have the greatest stake in maintaining a sound national economy. In their role as citizens, they can be strong proponents of such an economy if sufficiently aroused, and businessmen should remind them of that fact.

# TOWARD A MORE CONSTRUCTIVE ANNUAL MEETING •

FREDERICK N. ROBINSON

THE INCIDENTS WHICH HAVE TAKEN place at a number of share owner meetings in recent years and the adverse publicity they have received present a major challenge to those who believe that the annual meeting can and must be an important, constructive, and worthwhile part of any effective investor relations program. The increasingly frequent appearances of a small but constantly growing number of self-appointed share owner representatives who act as professional hecklers of management have seriously jeopardized the constructive results which management, the share owners generally, and the professional investors desire. The conduct and disruptive antics of this group have raised serious questions as to whether in today's environment the annual meeting can be made to serve an effective purpose or whether it will become a problem-riddled public spectacle. Nevertheless, I am convinced that a sound annual meeting presents unique and valuable opportunities to management and that we must and can creatively develop solutions to these problems.

## THE DEVELOPMENT OF THE MEETING

A look at how today's meeting came into being may help achieve a better understanding of how—primarily through errors of omission—the problems were first created and then permitted to grow to outlandish proportions. The first phase in the development of today's meeting occurred during the years prior to World War II, and for several years

FREDERICK N. ROBINSON is Consultant—Share Owner Relations, General Electric Company, New York, New York.

thereafter. It was characterized by small, routine meetings devoted almost exclusively to fulfilling the legal obligations of voting for directors and any necessary proposals. Few, if any, attempts were made to communicate freely information about the business even to the handful of share owners present, nor were there many attempts to communicate the proceedings of the meeting to the vast majority who were absent.

This has often been referred to as the "meeting in a phone booth" era. Except in rare cases, share owners were not encouraged to attend, and if they did appear, they were often ignored. The attitude which prevailed was one of "If you don't like it, you can sell your stock." Of course, the inevitable occurred. A few share owners revolted over this lack of concern for the participation of the owners in the meeting. Lewis D. Gilbert and others began their campaigns for share owner democracy, and their activities have brought the problem forcibly to the attention of the managements of many companies, both large and small.

But it was not until some years later that the annual meeting began to play its proper, important role in good management-share owner relations. The beginning of this second phase in the development of the meeting dates back to the late 1940's and coincided with the generally greater concern of managements for all aspects of their relations with the share owners. They became increasingly aware of their very special responsibility toward their share owners and the need to demonstrate—by policies, actions, and words—a diligent and integrated concern for the rights, needs, and interests of share owners. In addition, management generally became more conscious of the need to support broad stock ownership as a keystone of the economic system. I believe they also wanted closer owner-company identification to promote the mutuality of interests found in management's concern for the successful conduct of the affairs of the company and in the share owners' concern for the security and profitability of their investment. And further, management saw the development of a closer owner-company relationship as one which has important economic benefits such as providing a predisposed market for products or a ready source of capital.

Thus management took a more critical look at share owner relations practices and saw in the annual meeting a unique opportunity to enlist share owner interest in the economics of the enterprise and to create loyalty toward, and support for, the business which the share owner participates in. It saw in the annual meeting a communications vehicle which could contribute effectively to the total public relations effort. Management began to realize that an informative, well-attended meeting could serve as a focus for a review of activities for the past year and as a point of departure for the future.

It was in this context, I believe, that leaders in the investor relations field deliberately set out to make the meeting truly worthwhile—to make it an event which would do the following:

1. Furnish concrete evidence of management's concern for the share owners' interests.
2. Enable management to report in person on its performance of its stewardship role and to demonstrate the caliber of executive personnel.
3. Serve as an opportunity for communicating important facts about the company to all share owners as well as the financial community and the general public.
4. Enhance the effectiveness of the post-meeting report and other communications which are directed to all owners.
5. Increase the awareness of share owners and share ownership in the eyes of management, employees, and the general public.

In short, the meeting would help achieve the total investor relations objectives of the company.

The achievement of these goals was relatively rapid. In the case of General Electric, the 1949 meeting attracted some 1,200 share owners, while in previous years attendance had ranged from 100 to 125, most of whom were employees. The invitation to the 1949 meeting was designed to encourage attendance. The agenda of the meeting was expanded to include a well-planned, effectively illustrated address by the chief executive officer and a special question-and-answer period in which share owners were encouraged to participate. To increase the share owners' knowledge of the company, product exhibits and plant tours were made part of the day's program. And since it was an all-day affair, an informal picnic-style lunch was served.

This approach proved to be extremely popular with the share owners, and attendance grew significantly over the years—in our case, to over 3,700. Many other companies, large and small, took similar steps to make their meetings as interesting and productive as possible. In each such case, attendance multiplied, and the annual meeting of share owners generally came into its own as an important aspect of corporate life. The press took a new interest in the meeting and in share ownership; coverage was extensive and favorable. Even among companies making no special attempts to attract share owners to their meetings, attendance grew markedly.

In a short half-decade, the well-attended meeting became a reality. The planning of the 1940's had begun to pay off. By 1955 there was widespread understanding and support of the management philosophy which had recognized the need for this change.

THE RESULTS ACHIEVED

During the last half of the 1950's, share ownership continued to grow—the 7.5 million in 1955 had just about doubled by 1960. The return of proxies by share owners, which increased dramatically during the first half of the decade, continued at high rates, and these proxies were for the most part extremely favorable to management. Annual meetings became increasingly popular and, on the surface at least, successful. And in many respects, they were successful in reality.

Year after year, share owners attending General Electric annual meetings indicated in post-meeting surveys that they found them a valuable experience. They endorsed the efforts to make the annual-meeting day worthwhile in terms of business information, greater familiarity with company products, and the opportunity to see what the officers and directors were like. Consistently, 80 to 85 per cent said that the main reason they came to the meeting was to hear management's reports of the company's progress. Likewise, about 50 per cent said they came to see the officers and directors in action, and almost as many included the exhibits of company products among their reasons for attending. All of these are sound reasons for share owners to attend and have played an important part in helping define the nature of the annual meeting of the future.

It is clear from our surveys that one thing share owners do at annual meetings is to appraise the way the meeting is run: how the chairman handles questions; whether he is reasonable and fair; whether he conducts the meeting efficiently and in a reasonable amount of time; and, of course, how effectively and completely the questions are answered. I would suggest that their appraisal of the meeting translates in some cases to an overall appraisal of management, pointing up the need for management to come to the meeting with its homework well done. A further discussion of the actual conduct of the meeting will be found in the following chapter by James A. Farmer.

PROBLEMS RAISED BY EXPANSION

But just as a well-conducted meeting can create favorable impressions, so a poorly run meeting can have adverse effects on the audience. As the expanded meeting became more commonplace, it received much wider press coverage and the problem of professional hecklers became more serious. A few publicity-seeking, self-appointed champions of share owner democracy, in the name—but not honestly in the spirit—of proper representation of share owner interests, began to take advantage of the captive audience provided by the meeting for their own personal purposes. They engaged in antics which were clearly uncalled for and improper at a business meeting.

This improper conduct was disruptive enough, but perhaps even more serious were the other abuses some of these people engaged in. They monopolized the floor at every opportunity; they did not hesitate to be personally abusive to the chairman and other share owners. More often than not, their questions or comments were irrelevant to the real business of the meeting or the company, and they frequently campaigned for some pet personal cause or some publicity-producing crusade.

Such conduct was not only difficult for the chairman to handle but was grossly unfair to the other share owners present who frequently and vocally objected to having their time wasted in this manner.

These antics—the unwarranted harassment of management and the utter lack of concern for other share owners present—by such egocentric publicity seekers continued and seemed to reach a peak in 1962. After the 1962 meeting season was over, a magazine article asked the question: "Are Annual Meetings Really Necessary?"[1] It reported that a few thoughtful executives still insisted that the annual meeting idea was basically sound. "Even if stockholders ask silly questions," one board chairman was quoted as saying, "the annual meeting is their one day in court. They deserve to be taken seriously." But the basic tenor of the article was that many top executives have come to doubt the value of annual meetings and to feel that annual meetings are becoming empty "rites of spring" that celebrate but do not add meaning to stock ownership. The article added: "But privately, many responsible executives think the day is coming, when, like 18th-century medicine, annual meetings will do more harm than good."

## THE SEARCH FOR SOLUTIONS

What went wrong in the development of annual meeting practices which permitted the hecklers freedom to be so disruptive? What will be the role of future meetings? Will it be possible to hold a truly business-oriented meeting, one to which share owners come to learn the future plans and prospects of their company's business—both good and bad? How can meetings be held that will encourage serious business questions from the floor—questions more like those received daily from security analysts and other thoughtful share owners. How can we avoid at the same time having meetings disrupted by the hecklers?

[1]*Forbes Magazine,* May 15, 1962.

In planning our 1963 annual meeting, we tried to consider everything that we could do to help turn the tide toward a more constructive meeting. What, at least, was under our control? Should we skip the box lunch and product exhibits or eliminate plant open houses or forego the formal presentations by management or discontinue having the officers and directors at the meeting?

Any or all of these things would be easy to do—but would they be the right things to do? Would they accomplish our objectives, or would they simply drive more share owners into the hecklers' camp and simultaneously give some government agency ammunition it would welcome in order to show a need for more governmental control of business?

While we asked these questions about the future, we examined past practices for a clue to what our next move should be. Maybe part of the problem stemmed from having become too preoccupied with the related activities—lunches, tours, exhibits—while neglecting the business-economic content of the meeting itself. Perhaps this tended to create a holiday atmosphere which was bound to attract the exhibitionists. Maybe our efforts to be cordial and friendly to the share owners resulted in a tendency to be too lax in enforcing reasonable rules with respect to the conduct of the share owners at the meeting. We may have been guilty of merely attracting large numbers of individual share owners, without also encouraging attendance and participation by the highly business-oriented professional investors, thereby creating a vacuum to be largely filled by a few vocal and vociferous, though less knowledgeable, share owners.

### A NEW PROGRAM ADOPTED

After considerable study, it was concluded that every effort should be made to make the 1963 meeting as interesting and informative as possible and to continue the practice of encouraging widespread share owner attendance and participation but, at the same time, to take deliberate action to improve the content of the meeting and make it more businesslike and constructive.

In keeping with our practice of moving the annual meeting location to different parts of the country to enable more and different share owners to participate, San Francisco was selected for the 1963 meeting. We sent our usual letter of invitation encouraging share owners to attend. We used the best possible facility in San Francisco—one which was centrally located so that it could be reached conveniently by the largest number of share owners.

As in the past, the officers and directors were in attendance. We continued the practice of having extensive press coverage. Although we had no manufacturing facilities in the city of San Francisco, a number of plant open houses were held in the Bay area so that the share owners had an opportunity to see company product displays, manufacturing installations, and research facilities.

But most important in the long run were the steps taken to improve the tone and content of the meeting. These actions ranged from minor changes in emphasis in some of the details of the meeting plan and format to extensive efforts to encourage attendance and participation at the meeting by a number of security analysts.

Since in the past it seemed that some share owners missed, ignored, or failed to understand the order of business, careful attention was given to the agenda for this meeting. Each share owner was given a printed copy of the agenda with each item of business numbered so that he could easily follow the progress of the meeting. And to eliminate any possibility of misunderstanding, the chairman identified each item of business by number as the meeting progressed. The proxy statement was also given out for reference during the discussion of the proposals to be voted upon.

Special emphasis was placed on business economic content in the management presentations, which were specifically directed to the audience's interests as share owners and as participants in the private enterprise system. And in order that the share owners could see and hear a greater number of management people, the chairman made a point of referring questions from the floor to the appropriate company officers.

In previous years, little or no effort was made to encourage attendance by security analysts, and in general they did not attend the annual meetings of large companies. Whether this absence of interest on their part was due primarily to the lack of useful and informative material at the meetings was not known, but it was apparent that they would not attend our meeting unless we took some positive steps to encourage them.

Each of the more than one hundred analysts who regularly call on the company was contacted either in person or by telephone so that we could invite him to the meeting and discuss with him in considerable depth our philosophy about annual meetings. And from these discussions—most of which lasted from three-quarters of an hour to an hour—there developed widespread agreement and understanding of the importance of annual meetings and the need to get them back on the right track, not only from the standpoint of the company and the individual share owner but from the standpoint of most financial intermediaries as well.

We tried to point out the special opportunities the meeting could offer to the analysts, especially since there would be more business and economic content in management's presentations than was previously the case. We emphasized that only once a year did they have a chance as analysts to see every member of the executive office and all of our key vice presidents and directors all assembled in one place. This, we indicated, was also their chance to ask questions about the business and have them answered by the officers who had the key responsibilities in each area. And many of the analysts recognized that this could be a valuable experience. Realizing that a company cannot usually afford to take its key people away from their jobs several times a year just to talk to analysts, they saw that the kind of meeting we were trying to hold would be of at least potential benefit to them, as well as to thoughtful individual share owners.

It also became apparent that the meeting could be of significant help to the analysts in performing one of the more important but often most difficult evaluations—that of a company's management personnel. Here was an opportunity for them to get a better idea of the ability, character, and versatility of the top management team.

Because our meeting was being held in San Francisco and so many of the analysts were located in the East, we were aware that many of them could not successfully justify the cost their firms would incur for a trip across the country for just this one purpose. (In line with our practice in recent years, we did not pay transportation or living expenses for financial analysts.) By coordinating the annual meeting trip with another of our regular activities for analysts, we felt certain that a reasonable number of them would be willing to make the investment in both time and money. Each quarter for the past two years, we had held a plant tour and management conference for small groups of analysts at our Atomic Power Equipment Department headquarters and major facilities in San Jose and at our Computer Department at Phoenix. By scheduling these tours on the two days following our annual meeting, we not only made the annual-meeting trip more economically feasible for the analysts but also provided them an opportunity to focus their attention on two new and important businesses of the company. And, in addition, some of them took advantage of their trip to call on other companies in the San Francisco Bay area or elsewhere on the West Coast.

Almost all of the analysts with whom we discussed these matters agreed with our theory of the case—that the meetings had to be changed—and that this was a worthwhile approach to accomplishing the desired end. A total of 54 of them demonstrated their belief in the idea by attending the 1963 annual meeting, and most of these came from east of Chicago.

Several of them participated in the meeting, asking questions on such matters as the index of company prices, technical considerations concerning our participation in the Apollo contract, and the impact of changes in the economic climate of the European Common Market. These were good questions asked by professionals. They were more technical and business-oriented than most questions at previous meetings.

### A SUCCESSFUL CONCLUSION

All of these factors contributed to the meeting, which attracted a total of 1,717 share owners and turned out to be very interesting. While this number is less than attended the previous meeting in Schenectady, it actually represents about the same proportion of share owners in the area. This relatively large attendance tends to confirm the fact that the share owners come for good business reasons and that it is not necessary to provide inducements such as lunch to attract them.

Although we had some fear in the early planning stages that the more technical discussions might be of little interest to the less sophisticated share owner, our survey showed that 95 per cent of the audience was interested in such financially oriented questions, and two-thirds of these indicated that they would like more of the same. When asked to rate the business-oriented management presentations, over 90 per cent of the share owners ranked them excellent or good. When asked their overall reaction to the meeting, 95 per cent said they considered it worthwhile and their time well spent. One share owner commented: "It was my first opportunity to confirm the opinion formed by reading reports. I feel 'closer' to the company. The participation of management other than directors and officers at the speakers' table was most informative, and I would suggest more of this." Another share owner said, "During the better than 30 years my family has owned stock in General Electric we have been pleased with management. However, meeting these men, even if it is simply seeing them rise at an annual meeting, means far more than qualifications listed beside a picture." And, finally, a share owner summed it all up very well when he said, "Thank you for holding this meeting in San Francisco. It was informative, educational, and well worth attending."

Commenting on our meeting, the business editor for the *San Jose News,* after referring to the problems cited in the *Forbes Magazine* article, reported as follows: "Not only the stockholders but the company and the American free enterprise idea had a day in court at the G. E. San Francisco meeting." In summarizing his reaction to the meeting he said, "It was readily apparent that these were not 'economic royalists' parading their prerogatives. The atmosphere was that of men entrusted with a stewardship reporting with dignity and pride the accomplishments of the previous year."

These reactions from share owners, security analysts, and the press indicate some measure of success in this first effort to make the annual meeting a more constructive part of our investor relations program. Of considerable importance was the reaction of that key and important "public" that every one of us has—the executive office. The officers of the company who actually presided at the meeting were pleased and gratified at the constructive atmosphere, particularly as contrasted with the experiences of recent years. In closing the meeting, the chairman praised those participating in the discussion periods for their "penetrating and illuminating and interesting" questions and comments.

The total results of this meeting were encouraging. They indicate that as we are able to put more business and economic content into future meetings, we will eliminate the void which so often in the past has been filled by the so-called hecklers. This does not mean that we have found a magic cure-all or that we feel that attendance and participation by critics of management has been eliminated. Indeed, our meeting this year was not free from honest criticism and disagreement: there was discussion from the floor questioning specific management policies and practices and expressions of disagreement on such matters as stock options and their value to the business. But these discussions did not dominate, disrupt, or set a discordant tone for the meeting.

The experience gained in coping with these problems this year justifies an increased optimism about the future role of the annual meeting. As other companies, which are working for the creative development of even more constructive annual meetings, bring their talents to bear on the problems at hand, additional progress will be made.

So long as management retains its stewardship of the business, it must give an accounting of itself to the owners. A constructive annual meeting is certainly one effective way to do this. Benjamin Graham warns us to give this accounting by pointing out the following:

> In at least four parables in the Gospels there is reference to a highly critical relationship between a man of wealth and those he puts in charge of his property . . . a certain rich man speaks to his steward or manager, who is accused of wasting his goods: "Give an account of thy stewardship, for thou mayest be no longer steward."[2]

[2]Graham, Benjamin, *The Intelligent Investor,* Harper and Row, New York, 1959.

# CONDUCTING THE ANNUAL MEETING •

JAMES A. FARMER

UNTIL RECENT YEARS, QUESTIONS relating to the conduct of stockholders' meetings were of little significance. Before that time few stockholders attended annual meetings, and it was most unusual for anyone to participate except management representatives, who voted the proxies in rapid order on the election of directors and on other matters that happened to be on the agenda.

Although the greater number of annual meetings may still be of this type, those of an increasing number of corporations are attracting far more attention and much larger attendance than in years gone by. Such corporations as Standard Oil of New Jersey, General Electric Company, and American Telephone and Telegraph Company have had several thousand stockholders at their meetings. The wider distribution of stock and the efforts on the part of the companies to make the meetings interesting have helped to bring this about.

When the chairman takes the platform to preside over one of these present-day stockholders' meetings, he can assume that he is going to be confronted with some interesting problems. At a recent meeting of our company, for example, a stockholder got up and demanded the right to speak from the chairman's lectern rather than from one of the platforms that had been set up for the use of stockholders. The chairman had all of his papers on the lectern, but the stockholder insisted. Since he was the owner of six times as many shares as the chairman, he said he had six times as much right to use the lectern. At another one of our meetings a motion for a recess was made shortly after the meeting got under way. As it was obvious that neither the chairman nor the other stockholders favored such a recess, the motion was coupled with a demand for a stock vote. Such a vote at our meetings requires about 45 minutes; so that if the demand had been granted, the recess would automatically have resulted. Another meeting was interrupted by blasts from a bullhorn.

---

JAMES A. FARMER is General Solicitor, American Telephone and Telegraph Company, New York, New York.

At various meetings, obscure parliamentary motions have been made, sometimes accompanied by the claim that under generally accepted rules of parliamentary procedure the motions were not debatable.

It is sometimes assumed, even by those responsible for the conduct of stockholders' meetings, that the rules of parliamentary procedure contained in such works as *Robert's Rules of Order* must be followed at stockholders' meetings. The fact is that these rules, which are commonly followed at other types of meetings, are not binding at stockholders' meetings and are not well adapted to them. This is because the rules of parliamentary procedure, as the name indicates, were designed for meetings of a very different character—namely, parliamentary or legislative meetings. The rules originated with the procedures of the British Parliament. The comparable rules of the United States Congress are in essence the rules prepared by Thomas Jefferson for the Senate and published in 1801.

Luther S. Cushing and Henry M. Robert and others adapted the rules of parliamentary procedure to deliberative meetings of organizations such as religious, educational, fraternal, and similar groups. Cushing, a lawyer, published his manual in 1846; Robert was a U.S. Army engineer, and his rules were published in 1876. Both adopted as much of the congressional procedure as they thought would be suitable for these other types of deliberative meetings.

But Cushing and Robert devised their rules for meetings which in certain essentials were similar to legislative meetings—in that each member present had one vote, business originated at the meeting itself, and votes were taken after debate had been held for the purpose of influencing opinion. Rules derived from parliamentary procedure are well suited to such meetings.

Stockholders' meetings are, of course, very different from these deliberative assemblies. Voting is by shares rather than per capita, and voting by proxy is authorized. Because of the provisions of the proxy rules of the Securities and Exchange Commission and of state corporation laws, the matters to be decided at the meeting are fixed beforehand. The proxy rules are particularly directed to the principle that nothing of importance should be acted upon at a stockholders' meeting unless dealt with in the proxy material. Moreover, even the final vote on these matters is to all intents and purposes predetermined. Although there may be thousands of persons present at a meeting, they know that the votes cast by them will have little or no effect on the final result. As a matter of fact, most of them will have given their proxy to management and will not vote personally at the meeting.

When the realities of a stockholders' meeting are considered, it is not surprising to find a court in 1960 making this remark in answer to the argument that *Robert's Rules of Order* should be followed at a stockholders' meeting: "The plaintiff cites *Robert's Rules of Order* . . . as the binding procedure to be followed by any and all corporations while conducting a stockholders' meeting. This contention cannot be sustained."

Although the rules of parliamentary procedure need not be followed, the stockholder, of course, does have rights at the meeting which the law will recognize. It is his obvious right to require that a proper stock vote be taken on the election of directors and other matters appearing on the proxy. But he is also entitled to insist that the meeting be fairly conducted, and a meeting conducted in an arbitrary manner will not be free from the possibility of legal attack. In 1925 a New York court stated the guiding principles this way: "In the absence of express regulations, by statute or by bylaw, the conduct of meetings, including the election of officers, is controlled largely by accepted or common practice. The fundamental rule is that all who are entitled to take part shall be treated with fairness and good faith."

It should be remembered that the meeting is the *stockholders'* meeting. The courts have repeatedly said that each stockholder has a right to have the meeting conducted in good faith and with overall fairness. Recognition of this right of the stockholders should be considered paramount in conducting the meeting. It is important, for example, that stockholders at the meeting should be given a reasonable chance to be heard. Failure of the chairman to allow such discussion might raise the question whether the meeting had been generally conducted in an arbitrary or unfair manner and whether the stockholders had been denied the kind of annual meeting to which they were entitled.

In applying the test of fairness, however, the courts have not been guided by parliamentary rules. They have upheld action taken at meetings where the rules of parliamentary law were not observed but the meetings were conducted with overall fairness. On the other hand, they have held conduct unfair even though strictly in accordance with parliamentary law.

In applying the test of fairness, the courts have not been disposed to set aside action taken by stockholders unless the irregularities complained of had an important effect on the outcome of the voting. In the Fifth Avenue Coach case, for instance, a New York court refused to nullify the election of directors at an annual stockholders' meeting, although there was testimony that some stockholders were kept waiting so long by a screening process that they finally departed without attending the meeting; that some stockholders who tried to express themselves at the meeting were roughed up by a management employee; that the microphone was grabbed away from certain stockholders and then turned off; and that there were periods of yelling, turmoil, and disorder throughout the meeting. The court said:

> . . . both sides concede there was confusion in the meeting of May 8, 1961. That simple fact will not justify the court's interference unless from such circumstance we may reasonably conclude that stockholders' votes were illegally accepted or improperly rejected . . .; there was an unfair deprivation of the shareholder's right to make known his choice . . .; or right, justice, and fair play require a new election . . .
>
> In this case, testimony at the trial and a reading of the minutes of the proceeding reveal that opportunities were given to vote, though some refused to cast their ballots; that an opportunity was given to nominate other candidates for directors, though the sequence in the matter of procedure might be debatable, and that very few persons were in fact disenfranchised, whether intentionally or otherwise. There is no persuasive evidence that the result was affected or that the outcome would have been different if there had been an absence of confusion . . .

Another right which each stockholder has is to have the meeting conducted in accordance with the statutes of the state of incorporation. However, the statutory provisions dealing with stockholder meetings usually provide little beyond the following: (1) that prior notice must be given of action of an unusual nature to be taken at the meeting, (2) that at least a minimum quorum shall be present, (3) that stockholders are entitled to one vote for each share held, (4) that there may be voting by proxy, (5) that a certain specified vote is required to elect directors or to take certain other action, and (6) that the outcome of a meeting may be contested in the courts.

A further right which each stockholder has is to have the meeting conducted in accordance with the provisions of the bylaws. But this right is subject to the qualification mentioned earlier. The general rule seems to be that, even in the case of an irregularity constituting a violation of the bylaws, action taken at the meeting will not be set aside unless there is good reason to believe that the outcome of the vote would have been otherwise if the irregularity had not existed.

So much for the legal rules which govern the conduct of stockholders' meetings. They are buoys which mark a wide channel. The chairman of a present-day stockholders' meeting will always steer well within them. He will do so not because of any fear of the law. He will do it because he recognizes that the conduct of a stockholders' meeting is a business problem as well as a legal one.

Good stockholder relations, and good public relations generally, dictate that a meeting be conducted in good faith and with utmost fairness to all. Business considerations will prompt the chairman to avoid even a slight appearance of being arbitrary. He will not wish to disregard the more common practices which have grown up governing the conduct of meetings. Public opinion, much more than the remote chance of a legal attack, will guide his decisions in this area.

Business considerations, rather than legal requirements, will cause the chairman to encourage an open discussion of relevant matters brought before the meeting. Valuable business advantages can be derived from a free expression of divergent views. For the stockholder, it is an opportunity to participate, no matter how slightly, in the affairs of the company. Some stockholders get real satisfaction from getting up at a meeting and congratulating management or airing their particular grievances. For management, the meeting can be valuable as a sounding board of stockholder opinion. Management may well take action in view of criticisms or suggestions made at the meeting.

The chairman will usually want to be very sparing in resorting to the bylaws or to procedural rules in conducting the meeting. For example, he will be reluctant to rule a matter out of order even though that would be permitted by the statutes or the bylaws. He knows that in so doing he will take the risk of appearing arbitrary. He will not want his rulings to frighten off stockholders who might otherwise make helpful remarks at the meeting.

However, a chairman will be on firm ground in ruling motions or discussions out of order if they interfere with or obstruct the orderly conduct of the meeting. For this reason the chairman will usually deny a motion for a stock vote on a procedural matter. In the first place, it takes too much time. The meeting might fall apart while waiting for the vote to be counted. In the second place, on a minor procedural matter the chairman will want to avoid the voting of management proxies against the wishes of those present and will prefer to let the matter be decided by a voice vote. This is because such matters primarily concern the convenience or comfort of the stockholders who are attending the meeting.

The conduct of a present-day stockholders' meeting is more of a business problem than a legal one. Business considerations will assure that the chairman will conduct the meeting in such a manner that the standards of overall fairness and good faith are fully observed. This having been done, the chairman need not be concerned as to whether the niceties of parliamentary procedure have been observed. He can be confident that his conduct of the meeting will not be subject to legal attack.

# PROCEDURES FOR PROXY SOLICITATION •

T. HOWARD KEELOR

FOR MANY YEARS, THE SOLICITATION of proxies was little more than a measuring stick. With the creation of the Securities and Exchange Commission in 1934 and the introduction of proxy statements, it became a management tool. In time, it may well prove to be one of the most important tools available in the field of investor relations. Nothing can match it for prompting the share owner to write—certainly not the annual report nor even the popular post-meeting report.

Nine times out of ten, the solicitation of proxies is the responsibility of the corporate secretary. In short, his job is to produce the end product—support of management. With few exceptions, he looks first to the proxy rules of the Securities and Exchange Commission for guidance. Stock exchange listing agreements, state corporation laws, and company charters and bylaws provide further guidelines.

Only on rare occasions does the proxy material consist of anything more than the notice of the meeting, the proxy statement, and the proxy. With relatively few exceptions, the notice and the proxy statement are bound as one document. Many companies also send along an informal invitation from the chairman of the board or the president to attend the meeting. For the most part, they are bound with the notice and the proxy statement.

The proxy rules are specific about the information that must be included in the proxy statement. Certain information must be given when the annual meeting is one at which directors are to be elected. For

T. HOWARD KEELOR is Secretary, The Chesapeake and Ohio Railway Company, Cleveland, Ohio.

example, each such proxy statement must list in tabular form the aggregate remuneration paid by the company and its subsidiaries during the latest fiscal year to each director whose remuneration was in excess of $30,000; each person who was one of the three highest-paid officers whose aggregate remuneration was in excess of $30,000; and all persons, as a group, who were directors or officers. In addition, the estimated annual retirement allowances must be listed for the individuals named.

Certain other information must be set out in the proxy statement. For example, if action is to be taken with respect to the amendment of the bylaws, then the proxy statement must state briefly the reasons for and the general effect of such amendment and the vote needed for approval.

The rules also provide for the inclusion of share owner proposals in the proxy material if the proposals are submitted to management a reasonable time before the solicitation is made. For this purpose, a reasonable time is considered to be more than 60 days in advance of a day corresponding to the first date on which the proxy-soliciting material was sent to share owners in connection with the latest annual meeting. This rule does not apply to elections to office.

While the information that must be included in proxy statements does not lend itself very well to creative writing, there is no requirement that the proxy statement be a legal paper, nor need it appear to be. Indeed, it might well follow the lead of the company's annual report and have a little color, a few pictures, and a generous supply of open space. Among other things, the proxy statement is an invitation to support management—in person, if possible, and by proxy if not. Above all, it should be one that will prompt a favorable reply.

Proxies come in assorted shapes and sizes, although it is estimated that more than two-thirds of all the companies that solicit proxies now use punched cards. Among other things, the proxy form must (1) indicate whether the proxy is solicited on behalf of management, (2) provide space for dating the proxy, and (3) identify clearly and impartially each matter to be acted upon whether proposed by management or by share owners. Also, means must be provided to specify by ballot a choice between approval and disapproval of each matter to be acted upon, other than elections to office.

It is customary for the board of directors to designate two or three directors or officers to act as proxies for the share owners. Their names are shown on each proxy, and frequently they are referred to as the proxy committee. A signed proxy authorizes each or any of them to vote all stock registered in the name of the share owner at the meeting for which the proxy is solicited and generally at all adjournments thereof.

A proxy also may confer discretionary authority with respect to other matters which may come before the meeting.

There are two key dates: the date of the meeting and the date for the determination of share owners entitled to vote. Ordinarily, the former is fixed by either the charter or the bylaws. The latter date is fixed almost universally by the board of directors. More than likely it will fall somewhere between 10 and 50 days before the meeting—the period generally prescribed by law for sending notices of share owner meetings. While the proxy rules do not prescribe a minimum interval between the record date and the meeting date, experience indicates that anything short of 30 days is seldom ample for the solicitation of proxies. This is particularly true if ownership of the stock is widespread. To gain much-needed time, many companies, forced to struggle with a late record date, address and mail proxy material as of a "false" record date. This is an arbitrary date in advance of the record date, and it varies according to the time deemed necessary to do the job. Although this practice does "create" time, it also creates certain problems in the area of tabulating the vote. The stock exchange on which the stock to be voted is listed usually requires prompt notice of the fixing of any record date, and it is seldom less than ten days.

The proxy rules require that preliminary copies of the proxy statement and the proxy, together with any other soliciting material, must be filed with the Securities and Exchange Commission at least ten days prior to the date the material is to be sent to share owners. However, since the final printing of the proxy material should be deferred until the comments of the Commission's staff have been received and considered, the proxy material ought to be filed at least ten days prior to the date on which it must go to press in order to be ready for addressing and mailing as promptly as possible after the record date—or the "false" record date if one is used. "Preliminary copies" of the proxy material filed with the Commission are for the information of the Commission only, except that such material may be disclosed to any department or agency of the Federal Government and the Commission may make such inquiries or investigation in regard to the material as it may deem necessary.

While there is no requirement to do so, any national securities exchange is always pleased to review preliminary copies of the proxy material if the action to be taken will affect substantially the rights or privileges of any securities listed on the exchange, or if the action will result in the creation of new issues or classes of securities which may be listed. Such a review is helpful in avoiding actions or situations which conflict in some way with requirements or policies of the exchange. The exchanges can offer full assurance that submission of preliminary copies of the proxy material will not result in premature disclosure of the contents.

The availability of the company's annual report frequently determines just how early in the year the annual meeting can be held. Although ordinarily it is not regarded as proxy-soliciting material "filed" with the Commission, copies of the annual report must accompany or precede proxy statements if the solicitation relates to an annual meeting at which directors are to be elected. The general practice is to mail the annual report separately. However, in a recent interpretation of its proxy rules, the Commission advised that forwarding a proxy statement by first-class mail and simultaneously forwarding the annual report by fourth-class mail does not meet its requirements. If the annual report is mailed in advance of the record date for the meeting, copies must be sent to each new account opened from that time through the record date.

An estimated 75 per cent of all annual meetings are held during the first four months of each year. To partially relieve the burden that this places on its staff, the Commission strongly urges that preliminary copies of the proxy material be filed early and also that any material that is merely being updated from the previous year be so marked and that the changes be noted. When the changes are substantial, the Commission asks that they be accompanied by a full explanation.

About one-half of all the stock listed on national securities exchanges is registered in the names of individuals. Although they represent something in excess of 90 per cent of the total number of share owners, the solicitation of their proxies presents no particular problem, other than one of numbers. Almost without exception, proxy material is forwarded by first-class mail, and an envelope is enclosed for the return of the proxy by first-class mail. Some companies furnish stamped return envelopes, while others provide envelopes marked with a postage permit. Neither type of envelope has been able to demonstrate a clear-cut edge in producing a greater percentage of return. If the return runs as high as 84 per cent, the cost of postage alone will be a little less if stamps are affixed to all return envelopes. However, this should be weighed against certain disadvantages. First is the added expense of affixing postage to the envelopes. Second, and perhaps most important, is that they are not received from the post office neatly tied in bundles of one hundred as are the postage-permit envelopes. This is particularly important to those companies receiving upward of 10,000 proxies each day.

Perhaps half of all the companies soliciting proxies follow up their original mailing with a second mailing. To do this, two complete sets of proxies are addressed at the time of the original mailing. About halfway between the date that the original proxies are mailed and the date of the meeting, the duplicate set is matched against the proxies that have been received to date. The unmatched duplicate proxies are then forwarded to those share owners reminding them that they have not yet returned their proxies. A particularly effective device is a reproduction of a handwritten note over the signature of the chairman of the board or the president. Although the number varies according to the time they are mailed, a second proxy may be sent to as many as 50 per cent of the share owners. A careful analysis of holdings by shares may suggest a second mailing to only those who hold shares in excess of a predetermined number. To supplement the follow-up mailing, many companies ask their officers and employees to make additional solicitations through telephone calls, telegrams, personal letters, and personal visits.

An estimated 90 per cent of all companies conduct their own solicitations. However, there are some that employ firms that specialize in proxy solicitations. In some instances, the proxy firm's activities are limited to calls on banks and brokers. In others, they are limited to soliciting proxies from only those share owners who hold in excess of a specified number of shares. Still other companies use a combination of these limitations, and there are those who employ these firms to solicit all proxies. Companies that do not regularly employ proxy-soliciting firms call on them from time to time for special occasions.

The other half of all the stock listed on national securities exchanges is registered in the names of nominees, brokers and dealers, institutions and foundations, insurance companies, pension trusts, investment trusts, corporations, and others. The solicitation of their proxies requires special handling.

The greatest concentration of these shares is in more than 2,500 nominees for banks—and in some cases brokers and dealers—acting as custodians for estates, personal trusts, corporate trusts, pension trusts, investment trusts, and so on. It is estimated that nominees have the authority to vote in excess of 60 per cent of all the stock registered in their names. For the remaining shares, consent to vote the stock is secured in a variety of ways. In many cases, the nominee forwards to the beneficial owner an executed copy of the proxy for the number of shares owned by the share owner to whom the proxy is sent. It is accompanied by a request that if the share owner chooses to vote the stock, the proxy is to be forwarded to the management. In other instances, the authorization to vote the stock is returned to the nominee, and the nominee consolidates the authorizations under one proxy.

Because of the continuing growth in the number of share owners and in the number of companies soliciting proxies, the brokers' proxy departments are now faced with a staggering load in the first few months of each year. In an attempt to ease that load, the American Society of Corporate Secretaries, Inc., the Association of Stock Exchange Firms, and the New York Stock Exchange jointly recommended a few years ago certain procedures and standardized forms for the solicitation of proxies from the beneficial owners of stock registered in brokers' names. It is urged that brokers be notified of meetings as far in advance of the record date as possible. Although longer notice is desirable, ten days is considered an absolute minimum. The notice should clearly indicate the record date, the latest date for mailing the annual report, the latest date for mailing the proxy material, and the date of the meeting. This information is furnished on a double card, one half of which is used by the broker to report to the company the number of annual reports and sets of proxy-soliciting material that will be required.

In addition to a copy of the annual report and a copy of the notice and proxy statement, the broker also either forwards a specimen copy of the proxy or includes the text of the proxy in an accompanying form letter that requests voting instructions from the beneficial owner. Since the beneficial owner cannot execute the proxy for shares registered in the name of the broker, a postal card is furnished for the purpose of transmitting the beneficial owner's voting instructions to the broker. The form letters used by the brokers to request voting instructions are generally prepared and furnished by the company. However, some brokers prefer to furnish their own letters.

New York Stock Exchange member firms that have transmitted proxy-soliciting material to the beneficial owners and solicited voting instructions may vote such stock without instructions if they have not been received from the beneficial owner by the date specified in the letter accompanying the proxy-soliciting material—either 10 or 15 days before the meeting depending on the date the proxy-soliciting material was forwarded to the beneficial owner.

However, the broker can vote such stock without instructions only if he has no knowledge of any contest as to the action to be taken at the meeting and provided such action is adequately disclosed to share owners and does not include authorization for a merger, consolidation, or any other matter which may affect substantially the rights or privileges of such share owners. The card mailed to brokers prior to the record date ordinarily advises the brokers as to which matters may be voted upon by the broker without instructions from the beneficial owner.

Both banks and brokers are reimbursed for all out-of-pocket expenses, including reasonable clerical expenses, incurred in connection with the solicitation of proxies from the beneficial owners of stock registered in their names or in the names of nominees.

The percentage of shares voted is somewhat dependent on the distribution of shares. As late as ten years ago, most managements were pleased with a 70 per cent vote. Today, the figure should be somewhere between 80 and 85 per cent. If there is a controlling interest, it is not uncommon for the vote to be in excess of 90 per cent. Where it will stop, no one knows.

# REACHING THE BENEFICIAL OWNER •

RUDY L. VINCENTI

Nowadays it is not unusual for some corporations to have well over half of their outstanding stock registered in a "street" or "nominee" name. A share owner who chooses to have his stock certificates registered in a name other than his own is a "beneficial owner." If a bank is used as fiduciary, "nominee stock" is created. If a broker is used as fiduciary, "street stock" is created. In either case, the registered owner is not the owner in fact; he is the owner in name only.

Before explaining the reasons behind the increasing preference for beneficial ownership, several misconceptions—particularly those concerning street stock—should be cleared up. First, share owners who leave stock in their broker's name are not the traders or speculators they are often rumored to be. The stability of a broker's registered position as the securities market passes through its various cycles indicates this is not the case. In fact, this was particularly evident during the market declines of 1960 and 1962. What is more, the present tax structure and commission rates, combined with a more astute and better-informed share owner population, have loaded the odds heavily in favor of investing rather than trading. Thus brokers have consistently found themselves carrying large positions in industries characterized by stability rather than fluctuation—such as utilities, oils, food processing, papers, chain stores, and so on.

Were it possible to measure the holding period of an individual with stock in his own name as compared to that of a beneficial owner, we

Rudy L. Vincenti is Manager, Proxy Department, Merrill Lynch, Pierce, Fenner & Smith Inc., New York, New York.

might very well discover that the latter would be somewhat shorter on the average. However, more time and effort are required of the registered owner to buy and sell, and the difference could be attributed more to the procrastination of the registered owner than to the trading ability of the beneficial owner.

Another notion which is without basis in fact is that brokers coerce or persuade clients to keep stock in street name. This is not the case at all, with one exception. Where an individual is borrowing money from a broker—a margin account—he is required to deposit stock with the broker in negotiable form (this invariably means street-name stock) which is used as collateral against the funds advanced. Otherwise, brokers tend to discourage rather than encourage the use of the street-name stock.

The expense involved in keeping clients' securities can very quickly transform a profitable execution into a continuous liability. A broker's primary source of income is commissions derived from the buying and selling of securities for his clients; the cost of holding the clients' securities is an overhead item which reduces his profit margin. Brokers are required to render monthly statements to customers with securities on deposit even though there has been no activity in the account. The cost of sending out these statements, even for the most efficient automated firms, is over $1.50 per account per year, and most brokers find it far more costly than this. In addition, the cost of processing and mailing dividend and interest payments must be considered. The actual storage and safekeeping of the certificates is another expense. On the other hand, the cost involved in handling a simple purchase and transfer is considerably lower. In essence, it is the difference between high-profit and low-profit transactions. For brokers, however, the competitive nature of the securities industry requires that they offer this custodian service when requested.

Another misconception is that the decision by a shareholder to keep his certificate in street name implies he is not interested in developments of the corporation in which he is a holder or in the industry of which it is a part. If anything, he is probably more interested. In cases where detailed information has been made available upon request to both registered and beneficial owners, it was found that the beneficial owners consistently showed greater interest. Thus it would be a mistake to assume that beneficial owners are not interested in developments which affect their investments.

There are a number of advantages connected with beneficial ownership. A beneficial owner is a share owner who has chosen to avail himself of the convenience of having someone else act as custodian, collection agent, and bookkeeper for his investments. With very few exceptions, other than in the case of margin accounts, the convenience of having a broker or bank perform without charge and more efficiently all the services which the shareholder would have to perform himself is the major reason behind having street and nominee stock. If the stockholder has his stock so registered, he does not have to go to a safe deposit box every time a security is acquired or sold, he need not be bothered with registering mail, and he no longer has to be afraid of losing the certificates. His dividend and interest income is handled in any way requested—it is credited to the account, sent to the bank, mailed to the individual upon receipt or at a particular time. Moreover, the share owner can transact his security business away from home without being penalized for delayed delivery of certificates. His monthly statement gives him a complete record of his security transactions and investment income for tax purposes.

Nominee ownership also has certain compelling advantages over registered ownership. Certain charitable, religious, educational, as well as some social organizations prefer the anonymity of nominee ownership. Corporations avoid the necessity of providing proof of authority to endorse stock by resorting to nominee ownership. Similarly, trustees and guardians do not have to document their authority to transfer stock in each instance when a sale is effected. As trustees for many sizable pension and profit sharing funds, banks solve a number of problems for their clients by resorting to this class of ownership.

### THE DUTY OF COMMUNICATING

It is the duty of a corporation to see to it that the transfer of its stock is in accordance with the laws relating to stock transfers. The burden of proof is on the corporation, and it must bear the costs involved in complicated transfers. Most corporations now recognize that they must go beyond their registered owners to communicate with their entire share ownership. Provisions have been made for the proper solicitation of proxies, as well as for the distribution of all other financial information which is made available to registered owners. In so doing, they recognize that the degree of ownership—as well as the degree of market risk among both classes—is identical, and thus both classes of ownership deserve the same treatment and disclosures by the corporation. In the recently completed Securities and Exchange Commission study of the securities market, one chapter (nine) covers the obligations of the security issuer. The opening sentence of this chapter reads: "The keystone of the entire structure of federal securities legislation is disclosure." This statement implies that all share owners should have all the facts. There is little question that to differentiate between these classes of ownership is inconsistent with the philosophy of the Securities and Exchange Commission.

Nonetheless, there are some corporations which recognize only their registered owners. They feel no responsibility to go beyond the names which are on the transfer agent's books. By not making all financial information available to beneficial owners too, they are in reality denying their existence. Fortunately, such companies are very much in the minority. The decision to distribute information to beneficial owners is entirely up to the corporation.

In its listing agreement, the New York Stock Exchange requires that annual reports be distributed and proxies solicited from all owners. However, there is no requirement for the dissemination of financial information other than public disclosure of quarterly or semiannual earnings. Such public disclosures need be nothing more than a press release. Even the Securities and Exchange Commission has not specifically directed companies to make information available to a corporation's hidden ownership. Nevertheless, so that all investors would be able to properly evaluate their holdings, it is necessary that all segments of ownership be equally informed. And just because investors choose to have their stock in a fiduciary's name, the burden of responsibility is not shifted from the corporation to the brokers or banks. Brokers act as liaison between a company and the owners of street stock, but it is the corporation's responsibility to supply the information for distribution.

### COST: A MAJOR FACTOR

The main deterrent to a freer flow of information to beneficial owners appears to be the cost involved. Brokers ask that companies reimburse them for out-of-pocket expenses incurred in distributing corporate material to shareholders. In February 1952 the New York Stock Exchange suggested a reimbursement rate of $.30 plus postage per set of proxy material and $.10 plus postage per set of data material such as quarterly reports. Since these rates were suggested more than a decade ago, they do not reflect the increased cost of doing business. Automation in the securities industry has not offset the inflationary trend in costs experienced during the 1950's. As a result, some brokers have asked more than the New York Stock Exchange's suggested rate, particularly for proxy soliciting and, to a lesser extent, for the distribution of other financial information. Unfortunately, there is a distinct possibility that any increase in brokers' rates for performing these services will reverse the trend of more and more corporations supplying information to holders of street stock. Therefore, brokers should try to perform this service within the suggested rates of the New York Stock Exchange.

Corporations regard the brokers' requests for reimbursement as an extra charge; they do not recognize the economies they enjoy by having their stock held in street name. Transfer agents' fees are reduced by having a broker's name as a holder rather than the individual client's. Similarly, one dividend check takes the place of many. In the case of a stock split or stock dividend, a few certificates are issued instead of many. The company does not have to contend with changes of addresses. Lost stockholders become the problem of the broker or bank rather than that of the corporation. These are but a few of the factors which should be considered. Even when the fiduciary's request for reimbursement is taken into account, it is less expensive for a corporation to have its stock held beneficially than in registered form. In fact, companies which have made detailed studies of the subject have found this to be the case, although the amount that will be saved will naturally vary from company to company.

At the same time, the fact that corporations do save money by having stock held beneficially is not sufficient reason for banks and brokers to raise their rates above those suggested by the Exchange. Any savings a company enjoys by this type of ownership should accrue to the corporation rather than to the fiduciary. Reimbursement of reasonable out-of-pocket expenses should be permitted, but corporations should not be required to subsidize inefficiencies which exist in some financial institutions.

By the same token, a corporation should not attempt to effect economies by denying proper recognition to beneficial owners. Even though not specifically required by law or regulation, they should make proper provision for the dissemination of information and absorb the costs incidental to effecting such distribution.

Communicating with beneficial owners does, of course, present many problems. In instances where a company supplies proxy material and assures brokers of reimbursement, the New York Stock Exchange requires that brokers distribute the material and forward the voting instructions of shareholders to the company. Regulations of this type do not apply to all fiduciaries, nor do they cover all financial information the corporation may want to have distributed. It is not unusual for a corporate officer to be informed by a bank or broker that the bank or brokerage firm is simply not equipped to effect such a distribution. As reprehensible as this situation may appear, there are circumstances which, while they do not excuse such an attitude, do explain the position of these financial institutions.

EFFECTIVE PROXY SOLICITATION

The principal roadblock to the fulfillment of the fiduciary's responsibility in proxy solicitation is the fact that over 75 per cent of all corporations hold their annual meetings within the relatively short period of about 12 weeks, the so-called proxy season. While a company is primarily concerned with its own solicitation, it should be emphasized that financial institutions are simultaneously soliciting proxies for literally hundreds of corporations. As a result, a company must take the proper steps to insure that its proxies are effectively solicited. The most efficient techniques are covered by T. H. Keelor elsewhere in this book. While the mechanics are relatively simple, certain points bear repeating, because they are so important.

One of the most important steps is to notify banks and brokers that the company is going to have a share owner meeting. This notice should be sent well in advance of the company's record date. The New York Stock Exchange requires that it be notified as soon as the record date and meeting date are set—in all cases, at least ten days before the record date. It does not seem unreasonable to expect all corporations to provide similar advance notice to banks and brokers. If they are so informed, the fiduciaries are then in a position to advise corporations of their requirements so that they can distribute soliciting material to beneficial owners.

The New York Stock Exchange has definite rules which govern voting by brokers. When the Exchange regards the matters to be considered at the meeting as routine in nature, brokers may vote at their own discretion, provided solicitation material has been distributed to beneficial owners in sufficient time to allow them at least ten days before the meeting date to express their views. If no instructions are received, brokers are permitted to issue a proxy covering these uninstructed shares. This provision (the ten-day rule) definitely works in a corporation's favor when the items to be voted upon are designated as routine, as defined in Rule 452 of the New York Stock Exchange. However, it can cause unintended problems when the matters under consideration require specific voting instructions by beneficial owners.

Since about 65 per cent of all share owner meetings are officially classed as routine, stockholders tend to be lackadaisical on nonroutine matters as well. For one thing, beneficial owners have become accustomed to having brokers vote their shares regardless of whether authorization has been given. Despite the content of solicitation material, when specific instructions are required, beneficial owners often do not realize that their stock will not be voted unless they execute their proxy or authorization. As a result, a single solicitation through brokers will generate only about a 50 per cent response. It has been found that a second request or follow-up increases this participation. All that is required in this second request is a proxy plus a letter that reads like the following: "Proxy material has been previously submitted for consideration. As yet your voting instructions have not been received. Please sign and return the enclosed proxy; otherwise your shares cannot be voted." In some instances, a second solicitation has boosted representation of beneficial owners to as high as 92 per cent. Generally, however, it has brought an overall response in the area of 70 per cent. Thus it would seem advisable to plan a second request to beneficial owners on matters not designated as routine by the New York Stock Exchange.

The rules of the New York Stock Exchange and the Securities and Exchange Commission prevent financial institutions from stimulating a greater vote than that which the corporation's proxy-soliciting material itself can produce. It is the company's material and provisions for distribution that produce the vote, not the desires of the financial institution. As much as banks and brokers would like, they cannot go beyond an instructed vote in matters requiring specific instructions.

Brokers vote in accordance with the Exchange regulations, regardless of whether a corporation is listed or not. Unlisted companies should note, however, that the Exchange has stipulated that brokers are not permitted to exercise their discretionary voting authority where the solicitation material is not comparable to that specified in Schedule 14-A of the Securities and Exchange Commission. This provision may be interpreted as an effort by the Exchange to persuade over-the-counter companies to make fuller disclosures in their proxy statements.

Among other steps, in soliciting its beneficial owners, the company should make sure that its proxy material is delivered in proper fashion. This means it should be delivered in sufficient quantity, in plenty of time, and to the proper location. As already noted, a company's meeting is but one of hundreds during the proxy season, and human nature being what it is, priority will invariably be given to the easier-to-handle or, in this case, to the properly supplied solicitation.

It would also be helpful to notify the fiduciary of his registered position as of the record date. If the broker knows his exact position, he can vote it to a fuller extent. This will tend to result in a larger representation of street and nominee stock. Moreover, since a broker seldom issues a proxy more than ten days before a company meeting, it is futile to try to get it sooner.

While in some instances nominees' trust agreements allow them to vote without going through any of the formalities of obtaining prior instructions, brokers are not afforded this liberty. They have very positive rules and regulations to which they must adhere prior to issuing a proxy to a corporation for their share owners' meeting.

To re-emphasize these peculiarities of broker and bank solicitation, we should note that it is advisable to keep these basic principles in mind: (1) prior notification of the company's record date must be given banks and brokers; (2) materials must be properly supplied; (3) prior provisions should be made for second mailings where deemed advisable; (4) fiduciaries should be notified of registered positions; and (5) brokers' votes should not be expected any sooner than ten days prior to the meeting date.

### DISTRIBUTION OF FINANCIAL INFORMATION

In the matter of proxy solicitation, a company can tailor its procedures to satisfy the needs of banks and brokers, but when it comes to the distribution of corporate information, the fiduciary must take the initiative. Banks and brokers should be able to anticipate the publication of regular corporate statements, and they should be able to notify the corporation of the number of copies which will be needed for beneficial owners, preferably prior to publication. In this way, the fiduciary can reduce the time lag between distribution to registered owners and that to beneficial owners. Unfortunately, many brokers do not request material until they have received a copy as a stockholder of record. An equally large number do not request it at all. This indifference or lack of efficiency results in poor service to corporations and its beneficial owners. It is this failing which motivates many share owners to become registered owners and forego the convenience of beneficial ownership. They want to be sure that they will receive all corporate information promptly.

To get material into the hands of their beneficial owners, some corporations have asked financial institutions to state their requirements prior to publication; however, this procedure has not been very successful. How then are companies going to reach these owners? It appears that the solution to this problem must come more from the fiduciaries rather than from the corporations. This is not to be construed as a blanket indictment of all financial institutions. The majority do a very acceptable job as liaison between the company and its beneficial holders. There are enough, however, who have yet to bring their procedures up to standard. Until they come to understand their responsibility to both the corporation and to their clients, some problems will continue to persist.

Higher rates of reimbursement are not the answer to better communication, though they would reduce the losses most fiduciaries incur in distributing corporate information. A more likely solution would be to have the banks and brokers recognize their responsibilities and gear themselves to handle proxy solicitations and distribution of corporate material efficiently by providing adequate space, facilities, and personnel for this purpose. While most proxy solicitation does occur within a limited period of time, the increased amount of information released by corporations to its owners has made this less of a seasonal operation. Meanwhile, as companies recognize the importance of reaching their beneficial owners, they will be more persistent in their requests and thus bring on the needed modernization. However, like many other phases of investor relations, this too will take time.

Until this improvement occurs, companies will continue to have some difficulties reaching all their stockholders. Corporations can satisfy their obligation to beneficial owners by honoring requests for share owner material and reimbursing fiduciaries for distribution expenses. The competitive nature of the securities industry itself will induce banks and brokers to render maximum service in this regard.

## THE QUESTION OF HIDDEN OWNERSHIP

Upon request, a corporation can find out a good deal about its "hidden owners," short of their actual identity. For example, brokers can provide a geographical breakdown of the owners of the street stock, or they can give a distribution of ownership by size of holdings. Further, they can specify the type of holder who has his stock in street name. In fact, much more is available: with the help of brokers, a company can survey its beneficial ownership on such matters as product familiarity, corporate function and policy, share owner material, or even why they have chosen beneficial ownership. Although there may be difficulties in reaching or learning about these owners, the problems involved are not as formidable as they seem.

We must acknowledge that there are some differences between registered and beneficial ownership; however, these differences are somewhat insignificant. For instance, men are more apt to keep stock in a broker's name than women; nominee stock is more apt to represent larger institutional ownership than that in the form of registered ownership. Nonetheless, in carrying out investor relations programs, companies should not overlook owners of nominee and street stock. Insignificant variances, should they exist, have no bearing on management's responsibility to render an accounting of its stewardship to the beneficial owners, who should not be relegated to a second-class status. They should not be denied pertinent financial information which has a direct effect on the market price of their investment nor the opportunity to exercise vested rights as owners of the company.

By the same token, all fiduciaries must be constantly aware of their obligations. They should not arbitrarily shut off the flow of information to these beneficial owners. They should not increase their rates of reimbursement to the point of being prohibitive and must be prepared to act as effective liaison between the corporation and its owners. In those few instances where fiduciaries fail to fulfill this obligation, corporations are absolved of responsibility but unfortunately suffer the consequences, especially when soliciting proxies. A high degree of cooperation and coordination is necessary to bridge this communications gap. A little more awareness and extra effort on the part of all parties concerned could produce mutually rewarding results.

# AN APPRAISAL OF REGIONAL MEETINGS •

JOHN K. OTTLEY III

AT THE ANNUAL STOCKHOLDERS' meeting, management comes into personal contact with the owners of the company. The stockholders can see, hear, and shake hands with the men who are running the company in which they have invested their savings. The management becomes a group of human beings rather than a mere list of names in the quarterly dividend letter or a number of pictures in the annual report.

This is fine, but how can a company extend this personal contact to the thousands of stockholders scattered all over the nation who cannot or do not attend the annual meeting? A few companies in this country have found the answer in regional stockholder information meetings. One utility company reported that ten times more persons attended its regional meetings than were present at its annual meeting in New York. Another company reached over five times more stockholders in a series of regional meetings, which followed the annual meeting held in its service area. The real benefit from regional meetings, argue some officials, is the impression made on the stockholders by the post-meeting report.

However, at the conclusion of a series of regional meetings, one company official said he thought the idea should be abandoned. He added: "A much greater proportion of our stock is represented at one luncheon for mutual fund officers, stock brokers, insurance men, and bankers than we have in all our information meetings." He is correct if the company's sole purpose is to indoctrinate holders of large blocs of stock. If this was all there was to it, few companies could justify the expense of travel, hiring a hall, and the many other costs of holding a regional meeting.

---

**JOHN K. OTTLEY III is Public Relations Manager, Southern Services, Inc., Atlanta, Georgia.**

Other benefits accrue from regional meetings and the resulting contact with the "small" stockholder—and these are not easy to evaluate. For example, what price tag would you put on the following:

- A stockholder tells his neighbor that he was impressed by the courtesy and apparent competence of his company's management—that he "knows" they run a good shop "just by the way they talk." (One company asked those who attended its regional meetings if they found them interesting enough to discuss with their friends. The vast majority said yes.)
- A parent who attends the meeting goes home to his family with a better idea of how the free enterprise system works. He gives his children better answers to their questions about business. Maybe he even takes the time and trouble to discuss economics education with his school principal or school board.
- A voter is moved to write his senator or congressman about problems the company faces. (One woman sent an electric utility company copies of letters she had written her senators after a regional meeting. She complained that the rural electric cooperatives not only compete with the investor-owned companies but do so unfairly since they borrow money from the Government at subsidized interest rates and pay no Federal income taxes.)
- The press becomes more aware of the company. Soon the company begins to notice that more of its news releases are being printed.
- Stockholders take a more active interest in the company. This is indicated when their letters increase.

To be effective, regional meetings should be held in cities convenient to the homes of a number of the company's stockholders. The meetings must feature a top management team. Our company and at least one other electric utility company began by sending printed invitations and postage-paid return cards to all the stockholders. Their replies were tabulated, and a reminder card was sent out several days before the meetings. The stockholders were asked to bring the reminder card to the meeting—not as an admittance card but to give us an idea how many actually attended and who they were.

Extensive planning was done for meetings to be held in each of the seven major United States cities we visited. The hotels were checked in advance by a company representative, who made sure the meeting room was adequate, arranged for whatever rented equipment was needed, and so on. Then meticulous follow-up letters were written to the hotel managers so that all but the last-minute details were nailed down before the management team left the home office. It's a good idea to have one or two company people standing at the door of the meeting room as the guests arrive. A smile of welcome goes a long way in creating goodwill.

Companies which have held regional meetings seem to like the idea of having the chief executive and at least one other officer speak to the stockholders. These talks are often illustrated with slides. This is usually followed by a question-and-answer session which can be the most enjoyable and enlightening part of the program. Here the "small" stockholder expresses himself. The fact that management is willing to try to answer any question tends to create an excellent impression on those who attend.

It's generally a good idea to invite the press and actually visit the newspapers ahead of the meeting. One company got good coverage by exposing its top management to interviews in the newspaper offices prior to the meetings.

Opinions differ as to whether refreshments should be served. The meeting can be timed at an hour when no one expects to be fed. One company held afternoon meetings, and there were only a few requests for refreshments. Coffee and soft drinks can be provided at nominal expense and are generally welcome.

Stockholders may be encouraged to bring a friend to the meeting, but it's necessary to keep tabs on how many are coming so there will be enough chairs. Some companies set up displays and pass out literature or have literature available on the chairs or tables. A word of caution on the displays: they should be quite portable. Getting them from city to city can be a headache.

To get extra mileage from its trip, one company held luncheons for stockbrokers, security analysts, mutual fund and retirement fund officials, bankers, and insurance men on the day before or the day after its regional information meetings. Thus the company contacted holders of large blocs of stock and those who influence the purchase of stock with only one extra day in port, so to speak. The luncheon groups heard a condensed version of the presentation given at the meetings for small stockholders. The questions which followed reflected the greater knowledge of the luncheon groups.

The fact that questions could be answered without referring to notes left a favorable impression. To get more facts before the audience, the officers who presided at the question-and-answer session called on other officers to help answer some questions.

How many meetings should be held and how frequently? A series of meetings every three to five years seems to be frequent enough to keep old and new stockholders up to date. One company, with 65 per cent of its stockholders in a single state, held 15 separate meetings in communities it served in the state. Another company, with headquarters in New York, held its first meeting in Philadelphia. Judging that to be a success, it held similar meetings in Boston, Chicago, San Francisco, Los Angeles, and New York—one at a time. Our company tackled all six of these cities plus Denver in a single month. Among the things to consider in planning the sites are:

1. What are the major financial centers?
2. Where do most of our stockholders live?
3. Where do we need to be heard and seen?

Companies which hold regional meetings will want to know how they were received by the stockholders. A simple questionnaire can be handed out at the conclusion of the meeting or mailed to the stockholders promptly after the management team returns to its home offices. A postage-paid reply envelope should be distributed with the questionnaire. Multiple-choice answers should be provided, but we should also save a space for additional comments. One of the answers to each question should allow the stockholders to express dissatisfaction.

Our company received better than 50 per cent return of its questionnaires. The vast majority of the replies indicated that the meetings increased good stockholder relations; the stockholders learned new things about their company; the stockholders thought the question-and-answer session was interesting and informative and that the executives gave honest and forthright answers; and that the stockholders left the meeting with a greater feeling of confidence in the company.

That, in essence, is the why and how of regional meetings as expressed by a few companies which have held them. There are at least three conclusions which can be reached:

1. Regional information meetings are a logical extension of the annual meeting for a company whose management wants personal contact with stockholders who cannot attend the annual meeting. The post-meeting report suggests to all stockholders that their management desires this personal contact.
2. Replies to questionnaires indicate that regional meetings are exceptionally well received by those who attend.
3. When the costs of holding regional meetings are evaluated, we must remember that it is difficult to assign a price tag to most of the benefits of the meetings.

# REGIONAL SHAREHOLDER MEETINGS: ONE COMPANY'S SUCCESS •

WALTER R. BORIS

THE OBJECTIVE OF CONSUMERS POWER COMPANY'S stockholder relations program is generally to build a better understanding of the company's business and problems among its stockholders and in the financial community. It is our belief that such a program will primarily encourage a continuing and expanding ownership of Consumers Power Company common and preferred stock, particularly within the 65-county area which the company serves in the Lower Peninsula of Michigan, and in addition will enhance the effectiveness of the Michigan stockholder-customer group as a force for improved public relations.

To accomplish these objectives, the company has employed three basic techniques: namely, the implementation of regional shareholder meetings, open-house programs, and informative printed and spoken stockholder communications. The latter two programs are virtually self-explanatory and represent an effort not unlike the programs of most other utility companies. The concept of regional meetings of shareholders is, however, an unusual concept and one which we believe has created a relationship between the company and its stockholders which has benefited both. I am sure that stockholders who take advantage of our program feel that they have acquired a better basis for evaluating the company as a business, as an investment and—because of the nature of our business area—as a supplier of services to a satisfied customer.

## UNDERSTANDING THE BACKGROUND

To fully appreciate the importance of direct communications efforts with stockholders, the general background of a utility and particularly of Consumers Power Company should be understood. A utility has a

WALTER R. BORIS is Secretary and Assistant Treasurer, Consumers Power Company, Jackson, Michigan.

relatively large investment in physical plant. Normally, in terms of gross revenue, it requires between three and four years to turn over the investment. This fact, coupled with the regulation of rates by commissions, makes it inevitable that the utility rely heavily on outside money—that is, capital raised through the sale of securities. This fact alone makes it important for the company to project itself before the eyes of present and potential stockholders—not only the institutional investor—but also the "small" stockholder.

Consumers Power Company is a combination electric and gas utility which serves the greater part of the geographical area of Michigan. The area includes about 4 million people, of whom about 1.5 million are customers of the company. Annual revenue is about $360 million, of which about two-thirds comes from electric sales and the remaining one-third from gas sales. Add to this the fact that we have more than 85,000 stockholders, of whom 60 per cent live in Michigan. It is this latter fact which emphasizes the requirement for a total effort to communicate effectively with our Michigan stockholders.

It would be pertinent to ask why such a preponderance in Michigan stockholders exists. A part of the answer lies in the intensive efforts of the company, principally during the 1920's, to raise a part of its capital requirements through "customer ownership." In line with this policy, a series of preferred stocks were issued and sold to residents of the service area. Company employees were the salesmen, and their service customers were the prospects. Terms of sale were not attractive by today's standards but were in accord with common practice among utilities at that time. The preferreds carried rates of 6 or 7 per cent, and after discount to the buyer and commission to the salesman, the company netted about $90 for each $100 share.

Needless to say, sales were brisk; and when the company was ready to go public with its common stock in 1946, it found a large investor interest on the part of the public generally and the preferred holders particularly. The financing requirements of the period between 1946 and 1958 were high. From a base of approximately 3.6 million shares in 1946, successive sales of common stock were made until 12 years later, in 1958, more than 9 million shares were outstanding. It is obvious that such additions to capital had to be made at a cost calculated to place maximum capital in the company's treasury and at the same time offer attractiveness both on the basis of yield and security to the investor, all within prevailing market requirements.

This, we believe, was the case from the point of view of both the company and the investor. In fact, in line with a company practice of allowing employees to purchase stock remaining after purchase by holders of warrants evidencing pre-emptive rights, it has often been necessary to allocate shares to satisfy employee demand.

As a result of such stock sales, a pattern of ownership developed which led to our present preponderance of Michigan holders. The accompanying table summarizes this quickly. We cannot say for sure that this growth in the Michigan family of stockholders would not have occurred without the company's attitude toward shareholder relations. On the other hand, the result is before us; and if credit is due, it should be taken.

| | 1954 | | 1958 | | 1963 | |
|---|---|---|---|---|---|---|
| | No. Stockholders | % | No. Stockholders | % | No. Stockholders | % |
| Michigan | 35,893 | 51 | 46,872 | 58.8 | 51,475 | 60 |
| Non-Michigan | 34,227 | 49 | 32,675 | 41.2 | 34,300 | 40 |
| | 70,120 | 100 | 79,547 | 100 | 85,775 | 100 |

Aside from the dollar aspects of such a program, other benefits flow from the establishment of such a relationship, and these benefits can apply to companies not in the utility business—in fact, to any corporation or product where customer acceptance is a factor.

One of the harsher facts of life for most utilities is the certainty that they must inevitably petition to a regulatory body for rate relief. This is an action which is rarely ever popular with the consuming public, no matter how justifiable. Here then is a forum, a heterogeneous body of consumers or stockholders or both to whom we can go with our story. The goal is not to secure enthusiastic consumer approval of rate adjustments but, rather, to make certain that the consumer understands the necessity; and this we have done successfully to a degree.

One must agree that keeping friends while raising costs is a difficult job, but it can be done with a program of personal and friendly relations.

### THE REGIONAL MEETING PROGRAM

Since 1949 the management of Consumers Power Company has made a personal report to its stockholder customers in the principal cities which the company serves. Our company is organized under the laws of the state of Maine. At that time, Maine law required that the company hold its annual meeting in that state, and it was not reasonable to expect a stockholder to travel the thousand miles or so to attend. Further, our company felt that because the Michigan stockholder was probably both a stockholder and a customer, he *should* attend the annual meeting. Therefore, the annual meeting was to be brought to him.

Those first meetings differed little from our present meetings except in size, although the technique of presentation was improved as we gained experience. They differed from annual meetings only in the fact that the formal procedure was reported as an accomplished fact. Everything else —the presentation of reports, financial data, and other information— is a duplicate of the annual meeting.

The local division manager presides at the meeting, making whatever personal introductory remarks he thinks are appropriate. He introduces the guests from the home office. In addition, every effort is made to have present one or more of our directors residing in or near the area of the meeting.

The first order of business is to have the secretary or treasurer of the company report briefly on the events occurring at the actual annual meeting. We feel that this report should be limited in time to a maximum of two or three minutes and should only touch the major propositions and the election of directors.

Next, the principal speaker is introduced. He delivers the same report to these stockholders as was given at the annual meeting. He is always one of the top corporate officers—chairman of the board, president, or a vice president. The talk is carefully prepared to be a supplement to the information that is contained in the annual report. To the extent we can do so, we minimize the use of statistics, percentages, and other details on the theory that these are already given in the annual report and that repetitions would only lose the audience.

This is the real opportunity for getting across the message from management and for discussing frankly the problems of the company and the industry. After all, the shareholder probably already knows the gross revenue and earnings per share. He has come to look at and listen to the management, and his image of the company is formed by the management. He is interested in management's attitude and its approach to the company's successes and problems.

This principal talk should not exceed 30 minutes. It is usually followed by a movie, about 20 minutes long, which shows some of the past year's operations—for example, the construction of a new pipeline, installation of a new generator, or the erection of a new service center. Sometimes the films resemble a travelogue and show the scenic spots or business advantages of our service area. In any event, the films are all produced by our own public relations department from footage of significant events taken during the year.

At the conclusion of the film, the division manager again takes over the meeting, acknowledges the speaker and guests, and announces that the company officers will remain to answer any questions which stockholders may have and that all stockholders are invited to stay for refreshments. Notice that at the regional meetings questions are not called for from the floor. This is important, because we feel that a great many more questions are put to us in the friendly face-to-face meeting than would be forthcoming by microphone from a mass of people. And we receive dozens of pertinent, searching questions. Many, it must be admitted, are related to personal shareholder problems.

When we first held these meetings in 1949, a total of 1,500 persons attended four meetings. In 1963 a total of 6,000 persons attended 12 meetings. We became concerned about three years ago whether too many of those attending our meetings had become "regulars" to whom the event was a merely social one. We made a survey of attendees that year by asking them to fill out cards left in each seat. The results were gratifying. More than half of those present were attending their first regional meeting. This confirmed our belief that the meetings should be continued. If we can reach about three thousand new shareholders each year, we think it is worthwhile.

Careful accounting is kept of the costs of these meetings, including hall rentals, food, overtime charges of hourly paid employees, and preparation of the movie film and the various exhibits. A portion of these costs is recoverable in that the exhibits are used all year long at various company and civic functions, and the movie film is shown to hundreds of service clubs and junior and senior high school classes.

Our offering of refreshments is not elaborate. The usual rule is coffee, sandwiches, and cookies—although minor variations occur when a locality has some specialty for which it is known. Usually, the stockholders stay for about an hour after the meeting. We hold ourselves prominently available during the entire refreshment period—and many stockholders enjoy simply stopping to say hello.

## AN EVALUATION OF RESULTS

Are these meetings worth the cost and the effort? I don't believe there is a categorical yes or no answer. However, I do offer this: the question which we hear most often from our stockholders is "When will we have a chance to buy more stock?" This indicates success in helping to establish the interest of stockholders in continuing investment in new issues of the company.

We are convinced that these meetings help provide an informed customer-stockholder who is in a position to speak to others about the company. He may be able, as the occasion arises, to correct possible misinformation about it. In return, we feel that we gather much valuable information which helps us to put area problems in perspective.

A program of personal and direct stockholder communication such as that described here is by no means an infallible or the exclusive means of establishing a completely successful stockholder relations program. Due attention must also be given to other more conventional media and, by all means, to the other segments of the investing public. Most companies are very aware of the importance of a program directed toward financial institutions and security analysts. Our suggestion is that a fertile field remains in the development of a more personalized and more productive approach to the so-called small stockholder, particularly where he may also be a customer.

# SHARE OWNER CORRESPONDENCE •

WILLIAM L. PHYFE

CORRESPONDENCE WITH SHARE OWNERS falls into two broad categories: one dealing with share owner records and any required action by the company relating to security transactions and holdings and the other concerning all other matters of interest to share owners, which involve general policy matters and questions about the company's products and services.

Examples of matters dealt with in the first category are transfers of stock ownership, address instructions, lost stock certificates, failures to receive dividend, stock record information—including changes and corrections—and stock "rights" subscriptions (during a stock offering period only). Subjects which fall into the second category are too numerous to list, but they include anything from politics, community relations, and the American free enterprise system to company financial policies, operations, research, and product development. For example, letters from share owners who ask why they did not receive their dividend check belong in the first category, while those with suggestions that the dividend should be increased fall in the second category.

The first type of correspondence is most conveniently handled where the stock records are kept or are readily available. This would generally be in the treasurer's department in the company which acts as its own transfer agent. When share owners number well into the hundreds of thousands or millions, it is advisable to break down the work by type of case. For instance, separate correspondence units would handle (1) stock transfers, (2) lost, stolen, and destroyed securities, (3) dividend matters, and (4) record changes, inquiries, and miscellaneous matters. While many inquiries can be handled by form letters, large volumes of them require individually written letters.

---

WILLIAM L. PHYFE is General Supervisor, Share Owner Correspondence, Secretary's Department, American Telephone and Telegraph Company, New York, New York.

Share owner letters of the second type are by far the most challenging and interesting because of the wide variety of subjects covered and the various ways this correspondence can be handled. At first it might appear most efficient to refer letters to the various departments for reply, depending upon the subject matter; and this is often the procedure with customer letters. Although this is one way of handling the job, it falls far short of the objective of getting the most mileage out of this kind of correspondence. A better way is to handle such letters centrally under the supervision of one manager responsible for share owner relations who coordinates the information from other departments. In this manner, replies can be tailored to the share owners' interests and can be designed to enhance share owner relations.

The responsibility for these replies could be placed, as appropriate, in public relations or in the treasurer's or secretary's department. We have put the responsibility in the secretary's department; and because we are convinced of the importance of good share owner relations to the success of the company, all replies are signed by the vice president and secretary.

### A SUCCESSFUL PROGRAM OF CORRESPONDENCE

Many share owners are relatively uninformed about the business in which they have invested their money, and so our objective is to make them as well informed as possible. As a first step, every new share owner receives a letter of welcome to our share owner family from the chairman of the board. Among other things, this letter stresses the personal relationship we feel they have with the company and our desire to keep them informed about the business and what we are doing. The letter ends with this sentence: "When you have questions, we shall be glad to answer them; and we shall always welcome your comments and suggestions."

This theme is followed up from time to time with similar statements in the annual and quarterly reports to share owners. Then when a share owner's holdings increase and reach a certain size (say 500 or 1,000 shares), he receives another letter from the chairman expressing appreciation for the share owner's confidence in the business. Again we offer to provide any information the share owner may feel he might like to have; and we add that if the share owner has a suggestion, we would like to hear about it. Then in answering share owner letters, when appropriate, our reply often ends with: "We like to hear from our share owners, and if you have any further questions, just let me know."

The vast majority of our communications with share owners are in the form of reports, quarterly statements, other printed material, and national advertising. The information we furnish must, of necessity, be prepared for share owners in general. But when share owners write, this gives us an excellent opportunity to answer their questions on subjects of particular interest. The opportunity is twofold: improving share owner relations and keeping management abreast of share owner thinking and desires.

Initially share owners are friendly; and if this feeling changes, we feel that it may be the result of some shortcoming on our part. Replies to share owner letters that are friendly, courteous, and informative assist in maintaining and building good share owner relations. The value of share owner support cannot be overestimated: it is potentially powerful.

The importance of keeping management informed on share owner thinking is shown by the fact that every share owner letter addressed to the chairman of the board or president of the company is personally read by that official. In some instances, he personally signs the reply. To expedite replies on important matters, copies are immediately made and sent to the vice president of the department involved, while the original is sent to the secretary's department for association with any previous correspondence, and coordination with suggested replies submitted by the department or departments involved, drafting the reply, and signing the finished letter.

The letters are written in an informal, warm, and friendly style. We choose words which would be used if the share owner were present and sitting at the officer's desk. Perhaps the most important letters—those which require great care in answering—are the ones which express some dissatisfaction with the investment made. Here there is a real opportunity to change dissatisfaction into satisfaction. One share owner with substantial holdings expressed his growing concern for the equitable treatment of stockholders in relation to the company's two other major groups—the employees and the customers—during the postwar period of inflation. After receiving our reply, he wrote again in thanks and said in part:

> Your letter is certainly outstanding in its argument, its organization, its composition, and in its humanity and courtesy. It is certainly, too, an exceptional achievement in management-stockholder relations.
>
> Your letter has done a great deal to allay the concern we had about our investment, not so much, perhaps, by the facts it sets forth as by its humanity—the way it somehow conveys that you and the chairman of the board sense deeply, and with understanding, the situation, similar to my wife's and mine, of hundreds of thousands of individuals among your stockholders.
>
> We thank you most gratefully, confident that you are worthy of our trust.

In another instance, a share owner gave instructions not to vote his proxy for certain directors because their "shareholdings are so small as to raise doubt as to their interest in the company." While the letter asked no questions and did not require a reply, we seized the opportunity to write a letter on the subject of directors' shareholdings. The result is shown by the letter received, which said in part:

> I appreciate your letter and reasoning, but will continue to hold to my belief that the interests of the small stockholders are served best when they are represented by directors whose own shareholdings are substantial and who therefore have a direct, personal interest in the well-being and future of the company.
>
> However, this letter is not being written to prolong this argument. Rather, I thought you might be interested in knowing that I sent similar instructions to other companies with my signed proxies to them.
>
> Yours was the only company which went to the trouble of acknowledging my proxy. I think this is a perfect illustration of the outstanding way in which your company operates in the public relations area and makes me prouder than ever to be associated in a very minor way with your organization.
>
> My best wishes to you and the company.

This letter shows the importance of having, as an underlying objective in all correspondence, the improvement of share owner relations rather than an objective of changing the share owner's mind or his opinion.

Not long ago some share owners objected to furnishing their social security numbers. We received the following response to our letter explaining why the Government was requiring us to ask for this additional information:

> I am amazed and grateful that anyone, with as much to do and as many responsibilities to bear as you, should take the time to write me as you did. It gives me confidence that people still count with big business, even if we are to be reduced to serial numbers by our Government.

It has often been said that a good letter does three things: (1) communicates a thought, (2) gives the recipient some benefit, and (3) conveys a feeling. The importance in share owner correspondence of conveying the feeling that the manager writing the letter has a sincere interest in the share owner as a person and in his problems cannot be overemphasized. The examples above illustrate the value of this. It is well to remember that it is not the corporation but an individual person who is writing the letter.

There are occasions when it is advisable to answer a share owner letter by telephone. Telephone calls are appropriate when the inquiry needs clarification before an answer can be given, when for some reason a personal discussion is preferable to a reply in writing, or when the time element is such that a letter would be too late.

There are certain inquiries and complaint letters where it is best to have someone visit with the share owner for a personal discussion. In these cases, an acknowledgement is sent saying that "it is difficult to adequately cover your points in a letter and we feel that a personal discussion would be far more satisfactory. We have taken the liberty of discussing your letter with (*name*) and have asked Mr. (*name*) to call on you to arrange for a personal discussion at your convenience."

### TRENDS IN SHARE OWNER THINKING

We feel that there have been some noticeable trends in share owner thinking in recent years. In general, there is little doubt that share owners are becoming more and more interested and inquisitive about the affairs of the company in which their money is invested. In addition, our correspondence has reflected more than ever before a feeling of deep concern about political trends and events which they think may affect the free enterprise system. Share owners are worried about high taxes and the principle of double taxation of dividends. And there is more evidence that share owners are writing to their congressmen about these matters in support of private enterprise.

A great many share owners are sincerely interested in helping the company in one way or another. Many have ideas for increasing its revenues and earnings, which range from most unusual and peculiar suggestions to good ideas which are already in use or have been tried and discarded. Over the years, our file on stockholders' suggestions has grown most rapidly and is one of the largest. One unique suggestion was recently made by a loyal share holder of the fairer sex that we make available to women share owners a small locket containing a miniature replica of a stock certificate that could be proudly worn to display to friends. Other suggestions range from complicated engineering devices for products or services to activities completely foreign to our field of operations. All ideas and suggestions should be cleared through a single organization at company headquarters. This is highly preferable to having separate groups handling stockholder suggestions, customer suggestions, and those from the general public.

Other matters which have been the frequent subject of share owner letters are requests for general information. These include inquiries about the company's services and products, detailed information about stock and dividend matters—particularly about the possibility of larger dividends.

In the spring and fall we receive letters from high school and college students seeking help and information for term papers. They practically always explain why they picked our company as a subject; and more likely than not it is because they, their parents, or their teachers own some of our stock. Teachers and professors themselves often want material, such as annual reports and other financial data, for their classroom work on industry and financing. One share owner student asked so many detailed questions that it appeared easier to write his thesis for him than answer all his broad questions. Needless to say, this was not done. He was furnished with booklets, pamphlets, and so forth which covered his subject.

One inquiry which always brings deep satisfaction to management is from share owners who have decided to add to their holdings. Some write to ask if they can buy shares from the company. They seem reluctant to go through the usual channels and feel that because they are share owners they should be privileged to buy stock direct. Many are older couples who have some additional money to invest and want a larger dividend check each quarter for use during their retirement days. Younger couples, on the other hand, are often planning for their future by seeking ways to invest their savings for their children's education. These share owners are often particularly interested in the research and development of new products and services.

### CORRESPONDENCE AT ANNUAL MEETING TIME

After the proxies are mailed to share owners for the annual meeting, the volume of share owner correspondence skyrockets. Here we have found a real opportunity: first and always, for improving share owner relations on a larger scale and, second, for gaining an indication as to what will be on the share owners' minds when they come to the annual meeting.

Many share owners, when signing their proxies, add notes which are both complimentary and otherwise. Most of them do not expect an answer, and many notes are just observations and not questions calling for answers. However, we reply to all knowledgeable comments and in addition use the opportunity to express thanks for the return of the proxies, regardless of whether they are marked as recommended by management or not. This, we feel, has really paid off in keeping friends and fostering closer ties with share owners.

An analysis of the comments, letters, and notes accompanying the proxies has proved valuable in preparing for share owners' questions at the annual meeting. Although most share owners who write do not attend the meeting, their remarks are surprisingly similar to the questions from the floor by nonprofessional share owners at the meeting. Therefore, during the proxy period, management is furnished with regular periodic reports analyzing the correspondence by topics and showing a comparison with a similar analysis for the previous year. This indicates the current situation together with any change in trends from the previous annual meeting. In addition to these reports, information is available concerning share owners who say they are coming to the meeting, whether they intend to talk or ask questions, and in many cases the subject matter that they have in mind. If this material is properly organized and concisely summarized, it can be of great value.

## KEEPING RECORDS ON CORRESPONDENCE

What about the records that might be kept on share owner correspondence? Certainly a file copy of the letter and reply should be kept in some sort of a general alphabetical file of all share owner correspondence. But is this enough to get the best results from share owner correspondence? We think not, and we have some suggestions to offer on the matter.

A simple, basic 3 by 5 card file can be used to record the share owner's name, date of letter, subject matter of letter briefly summarized, to whom it was referred, and where it was filed. Thus we have a ready reference which tells us whether the share owner has written before and, if so, the nature of the correspondence. Cards can be destroyed if no entries are made for 5 or 10 years. This will prevent gathering deadwood in the file. The file serves the useful purpose of showing the nature of all previous correspondence and saves the time of reviewing the actual cases if they are not needed to help answer the current correspondence.

Copies of the replies to share owners can be kept in a three-way cross-referenced file: (1) alphabetical, (2) chronological, and (3) subject. This makes it quite easy to locate letters in the file with a minimum of information. From a practical working standpoint, the original letter is kept in the subject file, which may run from 500 to 1,000 different subjects, arranged alphabetically. In this way, there is a ready reference to what has been asked and said about any particular subject over the years. The life of this file can be maintained on a five- to ten-year basis.

Another helpful file is a "publications" file containing booklets and various printed material—such as officers' public speeches and the like—

that are suitable to send to share owners inquiring about matters covered in this material. This will contain much interesting and informative material on various subjects.

As far as reports are concerned, we feel they should not be a burden to make but that they are a valuable record of what has transpired and should be made on a timely basis. A monthly report works well: it appears frequently enough to be up to date and not too often to be burdensome. It might cover some or all of the three following categories:

1. Volume of correspondence:
   *a.* Unanswered letters on hand at beginning of the month.
   *b.* Letters received during month.
   *c.* Replies:
      - By letters from various officers.
      - By other departments.
      - By printed slip (for booklets requested).
      - By telephone.
      - No-reply cases (mainly thank-you letters).

   *d.* Stock-records matters sent to the treasurer for reply.
   *e.* Letters from those who are not share owners forwarded to appropriate department for reply.
   *f.* Unanswered letters on hand at end of month.
2. Nature of correspondence: broken down by subject matter of incoming letter and by numbers and per cent of total and indicating compliments or complaints as appropriate.
3. Time required to reply: percentage of letters answered within, say, three days, a week, or more.

With detailed monthly reports such as these, it is easy to summarize the more significant elements every six months or for longer periods. Since the subject matter of share owner correspondence during the proxy period each year is considerably different than during the intervening period, it would be well to consider making a detailed report on the various phases of correspondence during the proxy period and then summarizing the remaining monthly reports between the proxy periods each year. This provides a convenient record and a ready reference for interested management personnel.

While share owner correspondence is only part of our overall share owner relations program, it is an important medium in establishing a corporate personality. The share owner who receives the kind of treatment we have been referring to will build up in his mind a definite impression of the personality of the company and its management. And what is equally important, he will talk about it to his friends.

# MOBILIZING SHARE OWNERS FOR COMMUNITY SUPPORT •

JOHN E. CANFIELD

---

A FULL-BLOWN SHARE OWNER RELATIONS program has been a vital part of Wisconsin Power and Light Company's activities for some 28 years, and it is getting excellent results. What the company is seeking to achieve in this program is fuller public understanding of corporate plans, purposes, and programs; increased personal acquaintance with its share owners; and the active and sustained support of informed people who know and understand the company.

Depression-born, the program helped prevent serious unrest among share owners in a period when all American business, utilities in particular, was in serious financial straits. Because of the depreciated condition of the market, the company's preferred stock had sagged to about 20 per cent of its par value; dividends had dwindled proportionately. In addition, a state administration was seeking enabling legislation for the creation of a state-owned electric system. There were plenty of problems facing the company's share owners and management, with worry and evidence of hostility on the part of many share owners.

Meeting the situation head-on, the company decided to face its share owners with facts and information which they did not have and which they needed in order to judge Wisconsin Power and Light Company intelligently. Meetings were held in each of the company's 14 operating districts. Share owners were told why they were not receiving a full dividend and how they could help improve the company's income by

---

JOHN E. CANFIELD is Vice President, Wisconsin Power and Light Company, Madison, Wisconsin.

encouraging greater use of its services. They were also briefed on the adverse political climate under which Wisconsin utilities were laboring, and they were told that they could combat this trend by helping to take the facts to the public about the company of which they were part owners.

An important development of these initial meetings was the organization of committees (one for each district) to represent the interests of all the share owners of the district and to serve as a liaison between the company management and the share owners. These committees, which range in size from 6 to 20 members, still exist and are one of the principal strengths of the entire share owner program. Committee support and work were effective from the very outset of the program and remain a vital part of Wisconsin Power and Light Company's contact with share owners and the public.

Since the inception of the initial share owner relations program, meetings between company management and the district share owner committees have been held once or twice a year. Each meeting is fully reported to all share owners living in the area in a letter sent out over the signatures of committee members.

Share owner committees also follow with interest the company's advertising and merchandising programs, the general public relations events, the construction program, the progress and effect of cooperation with neighboring utility companies, and the service and financial progress of the company. Over the years, share owner committee members have become well acquainted with the workings of Wisconsin Power and Light Company and have shared this knowledge with all of the share owners they represent.

One of the principal advantages of our share owner organizations has been the part they have played in helping to bring the company's stock into the state. Before 1948, the preferred stock was largely held (about 85 per cent) in the state, much of it having been sold by employees. Before that year, all of the common stock was owned by the holding company. With distribution of the common stock in 1948, about 18.5 per cent went to share owners living in Wisconsin.

Through the general meetings with share owners, the periodic meetings of the committees—and the letters sent out to all of the share owners in their respective districts—there was created an increased interest in the company's common shares, and the percentage of home ownership of the common stock began to rise.

Two years after distribution, the percentage of common shares owned in Wisconsin had climbed to 30 per cent. By 1951, this percentage had risen to 49 per cent and continued upward until in 1963 the percentage of shares owned in Wisconsin was 66.3 per cent. The number of Wisconsin-owned preferred shares has always been large—about 73.2 per cent in 1963.

Not only has this broadened the base for company contact with its share owners, but through the numerous contacts there has been developed a sizable group of people within its operations area who have a dual interest—that of customer and part owner of the company.

Under our financing programs the common-share owners have pre-emptive rights on new issues of common stock. Normally, the preferred-share owners do not have pre-emptive rights; but because there is a good market for the preferred shares in the state, the company has also offered new issues of preferred stock to existing preferred-share owners. In some cases, the offering has been oversubscribed by them.

At times, when legislation before state or national lawmakers, if passed, would have seriously handicapped or retarded the progress of utility operation, the share owners have been very helpful in their letters, telegrams, and personal contacts with legislators urging defeat of measures as they see the possible effects of the legislation on their and the company's interests.

Share owners in numerous instances have played important roles in times of municipal acquisition action or in directing public opinion to support the company's continued operations in their local communities. During the early days of the share owner relations program, the company was faced with as many as 22 municipal acquisition actions, but none of the communities was lost to company service.

General meetings with share owners have been held periodically since the organization of the district committees. However, this activity was put on a regular schedule in 1958, when the company held a series of 16 meetings, one for each of the 13 operating districts we then had, one in Madison, and two in Milwaukee.

The company does not serve either Madison or Milwaukee, but because of the large number of share owners living in these cities, they were included. One meeting only was first scheduled for Milwaukee, but because of the apparent novelty of a general share owner meeting and the promise of information which these investors wanted and would receive, there was overwhelming acceptance of the company's invitation. It was necessary to send out more than 800 cards asking share owners to attend a second meeting which was hastily scheduled for the night following the first meeting.

So successful was the 1958 series of meetings, with attendance of approximately 6,000 share owners, that the program was put on a regular three-year schedule and was updated and repeated in 1961. Again there was enthusiastic and overwhelming response, with 5,500 share owners attending 15 meetings, or about 25 per cent of the share owners in the operating area.

It was believed that direct communication with as many share owners as possible would serve to supplement the information they receive through share owner committee letters, dividend enclosures, special mailings, publicity, advertising, the annual report, the quarterly reports, and by other means. The program was taken right into the home communities of the share owners: to a principal town or city, usually the company's headquarters city in each operating district. They were held in schools, churches, hotels, private and public auditoriums—where the people could gather easily from a wide area, they could park their cars, and facilities were adequate to handle the crowds that attended.

A central theme was selected and exhibits were carefully planned and executed to expand and amplify that theme. In 1958 and 1961, the central theme was "PEOPLE, POWER, PROGRESS." In 1963, it was "INVESTORS HELP BUILD AMERICA'S FUTURE." A central panel exhibit featured the balanced diversity of industry, agriculture, and domestic service loads of the company's service area. It also emphasized the company's ability to serve the loads. This exhibit also stressed the company's fourfold goal, which is a code of principles by which all company business is guided:

1. Customers: to provide the best in utility service at the lowest equitable rates for the territory served.
2. Employees: to maintain a high standard of working conditions and to pay wages in keeping with the size of the community and the success of the company.
3. Share owners: to earn and pay to the share owners a fair return on their investment.
4. Communities: to be a worthy member of each community we serve and to support and promote the American free enterprise system.

Supplementing the central panel display were commercial displays obtained from suppliers and other utilities. Some showed cut-away portions of power plants, which demonstrated the principles of electric generation. Others showed methods of transporting natural gas by pipeline, recommendations for insulating homes for electric space heating, an atomic power plant model, various pieces of safety equipment and tools used in electric and gas operations, and similar matters.

Displays of pictures showing various applications of electric and natural gas service proved of great interest to share owners. Selected literature covered electric and gas space heating, atomic energy progress, the company's annual report, and the industrial development program.

Talks by the president, executive vice president, vice president, and treasurer presented a phase of company operations. These were not carefully written and read; nor were they polished, generalized, or evasive. They were down to earth, off the cuff, understandable, and couched in language that would be familiar to nontechnical people. At the conclusion of the talks, questions were solicited and received from the share owners. No question was evaded; and answers were given as concisely, factually, and completely as possible.

During the social hour which followed each meeting, refreshments were served; and the share owners met and visited with company executives, asked more questions, and expressed opinions. They seemed to realize that they were talking with men who know their business.

Newspaper people were invited to the meetings, and coverage has been very generous. Since the inception of the fully organized meeting series, there has been a noticeable increase in the volume of general company publicity used throughout the year.

On the basis of the fine response to the general meeting part of our share owner program in 1958, it was firmly established that this was a workable and much-needed type of program that could be continued on a regular three-year basis. The 1961 series, an improvement on the earlier program, again provided company management with the opportunity to again meet with large groups of share owners and to present the updated company story.

Following the 1961 series of meetings, our share owner relations program received nationwide recognition through four important awards. These awards included the Silver Anvil Award of the Public Relations Society of America and awards from the Wisconsin Chapter of the Public Relations Society of America, National Securities Trader's Association, and the United Shareowners of America, Inc. This recognition is interpreted as evidence that the company's program is a type of activity which could be of great value to many investor-owned corporations under adaptions suitable to their operations and area.

Comparison and evaluation of the 1958 and 1961 series of meetings, and the encouraging reactions of share owners which continued to come in during the intervals when no area meetings were scheduled, led to the decision to make the share owner relations program a yearly sustaining feature with five meetings to be held each year.

Beginning with 1963, meetings were to be alternated between the 13 operating areas and Madison and Milwaukee, with all areas ultimately being on a three-year basis. Because of the new plan of scheduling, there was only a two-year interval for the five communities where meetings were held in 1963. However, the response was again as enthusiastic as it had been in previous years, and the 1963 attendance was 27.1 per cent of all the share owners in the five areas where meetings were held.

While the general meetings for share owners serve to stimulate greater interest in and understanding of Wisconsin Power and Light Company, and also serve as a measuring device of share owner attitudes, a most important part of the entire program is the sustained interest and work of the 13 share owner committees. Invitations for the general meetings are sent out over the signatures of committee members in each instance, and these committee members are present at the meetings to greet the share owners they represent.

Now a part of the company's program for 28 years, the share owner committees have served as a vital link for communication with the public in general and particularly with those who are share owners of the company. Each committee is elected every five years by and represents all of the share owners within an operating area. Over the years, it has become a distinct honor to be a member of a district committee, attendance at meetings is good, and action on matters of importance is prompt and effective.

There has been no lessening of other forms of share owner or public relations activities because of the success of the committee groups or the area share owner meetings. We feel that all of the various methods of public contact—together with the normal good relations created by courteous, friendly, and efficient service—all are necessary to a well-rounded program.

Employees of the company also get a different look at the share owner-customer. They are made aware of the importance of the share owner who has invested his money so that we can buy the trucks, tools, and equipment that are being used and operated by employees. His friends and customers identify themselves to the employee as share owners and give him credit for a job well done or are critical of inefficiencies.

These share owner-customers ask employees questions about company matters—about dividends, new stock, or where the invested money is being spent and for what purposes. Employees are placed in the position of answering the questions, and they get the feel of these persons who have invested their money in the company.

It must be remembered that every person—regardless of his name, age, financial standing, or occupation—has his own sphere of influence and is important to someone. It is the experience of most corporations that the majority of their share owners are small investors. But it takes a great many small investors to meet the financial requirements of a utility company.

Each share owner, however, has a voice that can be raised in behalf of the company he owns. As these voices increase in volume, the company story reaches farther out into the places where it is beneficial that it be heard. A good company has a good story to tell. It must tell its story in many ways—by sound business methods, by good operations, by good service, and by disseminating true and factual information in a way that is understandable and is believed.

We believe that the share owner program of Wisconsin Power and Light Company will have a lasting effect on the many share owners contacted and that the company will maintain and appreciably increase a strong grass-roots support for and understanding of the company.

# SECTION III

## *Investor* **Publications**

*One of the most effective methods of reaching all of those concerned in the ownership of a company, both individual share owners and professional investors, is the printed word. This has been substantiated time and again by companies which have taken pains to produce annual reports, post-meeting reports, magazines, and other investor publications of the highest quality—publications which are not only informative but interesting.*

# A WORKING PHILOSOPHY FOR THE ANNUAL REPORT •

J. HERVIE HAUFLER

---

FOR MOST COMPANIES, THE ANNUAL REPORT is a difficult document, a devourer of man-hours, an infinitely changeable creature given to complete metamorphoses even at the moment it is on the press, and oftentimes a major battleground of corporate policy. Much of this seems to be natural and healthy, for in its evolution upward from the dry-as-dust accounting statement, the annual report has become the most important and intimate expression of many companies—the result of a determined effort to fix at a given moment in time an accurate likeness of a complex and fast-changing corporate personality and the product of a supreme attempt to catch on paper the uniqueness of the organization. It must be expected to come hard.

To produce such a document, each company obviously must develop its own formulas and procedures. Yet this chapter is written in the belief that there are common denominators and that, therefore, a review of one company's experience can have some measure of value for all. I am encouraged in this belief by several factors growing out of work on General Electric's annual report.

Those who have worked on the General Electric annual report have had the time, resources, and encouragement to develop not merely a procedure for getting the job done but a kind of working philosophy toward it. The elements of this philosophy obviously fit the efforts of a big company with a very large share owner audience and an "extracurricular" use of the annual report that has raised the print order to 800,000 copies per year. Consequently, there are undoubtedly elements that are not applicable to companies with much smaller share owner lists, and there may well be some that are appropriate to no other company. But for General Electric this working philosophy has eased the course for

---

J. HERVIE HAUFLER is Manager, Editorial Service Operation, General Electric Company, New York, New York.

the report's editors, for management, and for those who handle its production.

The main points of our annual report philosophy are a synthesis of viewpoints rather than an entirely personal perspective; they are offered as a description, not a prescription.

*A plan for the annual report.* The plan is nothing elaborate: it is confined to 10 or 15 typewritten sheets. However, the important thing is that the plan *is* typewritten and reproduced by multilith. This enables us to get the year's strategy worked out and approved in expendable drafts rather than in costly type—to get the main directions agreed upon before rather than after the expensive work of assembly, layout, and typography are done.

We try to make the plan as complete as the blueprint for a house. One of the elements is a review of our experiences in preparing the preceding annual report. From management's reviews of the report's material, we gather any thoughts or recommendations that should be carried forward into the planning of the upcoming report. Did the directors give any indication of changes they would like to see incorporated another year? Did security analysts complain about anything or have particular praise for an innovation they would like to see repeated? Did correspondence from share owners reveal any suggestions that should be considered? And what points arising out of opinion research need to be factored into the new report? All of these are in one retrospective section of the plan.

Another section sets down what we believe to be the "main currents" of the year for General Electric. In any given year a company does mostly the same things it did the preceding year, but some aspects of the business have been given special attention. Perhaps it is cost reduction—efforts to improve efficiency and pry loose the jaws of the cost-price squeeze. Maybe it has been a particularly fruitful year for research and development. Then again, the feature topic may have been organizational—major changes in the management team or new arrangements of operating components made to fit changing times, markets, and opportunities. One of the chief tasks of the report editors is to be sensitive to the main currents that characterize a given year and be able to pinpoint these in accurate language. The plan includes our first try at this. It recommends the theme.

Also included in the plan is the suggested paging arrangement and what is proposed for the cover. The plan describes the main ideas and illustration for each spread of the report and points out any major changes contemplated.

Finally, the plan includes a schedule: times and dates of all reviews and who will attend them are listed. The date for the first draft of the chief executive's message is specified. Important production dates are set —that is, when completed dummies will be prepared, advance copies will be mailed to directors, the report will go to press, and the mailing to share owners will begin and end.

The plan usually goes through two or three revisions, as management suggestions are worked into the text and as new information is received. But if we compare the final plan to the finished report, we find that the report is simply a carrying-through of the plan. However, we are not inflexible: changes are made and information updated right up to the press time, although the main outlines are argued out on a duplicating machine. No major details of the report come as a surprise or a shock to top officers: they have been forewarned by the plan and have contributed to its development. Late switches in direction are avoided, and no one has any excuse for missing deadlines, for they are all spelled out in the plan.

*A companywide approach.* General Electric is too big and complex for any group of men in a New York tower to report on sensibly and accurately. Those of us who work on the report keep up as well as we can by concentrating on assigned parts of the whole—that is, one individual keeps informed on a year-round basis about developments in consumer goods; another covers aerospace and defense; and another, utility and industrial businesses. Accounting representatives develop the financial portions.

But when the time comes for preparing the plan, we invite companywide participation. Each fall a letter is sent to all division managers outlining the needs for the forthcoming report and asking for their recommendations of achievements, outstanding developments, and problem areas which they feel should be considered for reporting to the share owners. We make it plain that the report's space is limited and that we have room for only the most important and significant developments.

The replies we get are varied. Some division managers give us their own assessments; some ask their department managers to reply. Others pass the job on to marketing managers or communications specialists. By one means or another, however, we amass the information from which the report is to be synthesized. This written material is supplemented by personal interviews, plant visits, and many phone calls by the report's editors and researchers.

Out of this research, we derive the main currents and first draft of the plan. We are then ready to go after top management's ideas. Interviews are lined up with the principal officers of the company. As preparation for each interview, the officer is asked to read the plan and be ready to comment on it. By the time a revised plan is completed, we have the advantage of the thinking of the uppermost ranks of General Electric.

This whole process is helped by the attitude of our officers that inclusion in the annual report is a sort of privilege. They are therefore particular about what specifics are included in the report. They know that a showy but trivial item will get knocked out. The examples and illustrations in the annual report have to deserve to be included. Thus there is a great deal of competition for representation in the limited space of the report, strengthened by the obvious marketing advantages of reaching 800,000 people. The editors never have to plead for interest and cooperation.

The finished report mirrors this companywide effort. Even though consumer items inevitably win higher reading scores than heavy capital goods or industrial equipment, a *balanced* perspective of General Electric requires that the share owner have some familiarity with these major parts of the business. We try to make his assimilation of these less personal areas as interesting as possible.

*Joint effort by financial and public relations specialists.* The editor-in-chief of the annual report is a public relations man, but his main team member is from the accounting function. In the early stages of development, the heaviest workload falls to the public relations representatives: the securing of pictures, the choices of design alternatives, and so forth are handled primarily by the public relations specialists. One way that accounting contributes at this stage is by helping to keep the right emphasis: we do not want to overplay minor items or underplay developments that had a real impact on the year's results.

In the later stages, the financial experts carry most of the load. Public relations representatives have been happily filling the report's pages with zeroes, but the time comes for these to be transformed into specific figures. Accounting accepts responsibility for the accuracy of the report, not merely in the figures but in the exactness of the factual information. Accounting runs its own independent check of all material in the report.

This teamwork is carried through at the top levels: the comptroller and the vice president of marketing and public relations are present at the reviews, including the review by members of the board of directors. The team preparing the report takes extraordinary precautions to guard against inaccuracies. We try, of course, to verify all the data in the text of the report before we set it in type and paste it in comprehensive dummies. After the preliminary pasted-up dummy is completed, reviewed with top management, and revised to incorporate its suggestions, we have 250 black-and-white copies run off. These checking copies are distributed throughout the company. The amount of corrections and changes which result is indicated by the fact that our bill for alterations runs well above that for the original typesetting as we and our collaborators throughout the company strive for the most exact wording and the most up-to-date facts. All recipients of checking copies are given a deadline for making changes.

When these have all been made and the type revised, we imprint the text on proofs of the color illustrations and bind these into finished-looking books. Thus management is able to see dummies of the report in color, very much as it will appear in final form yet at a point where final figures still need to be added and where further refinement and modification can be made. At the final review, by the directors, similar color dummies with the text inserted are prepared, but this time they contain the final figures. The editors make two additional thorough readings—at the typesetter's after the board changes have been made and at the printer's where press sheets are given the final O.K. This procedure is elaborate and adds to costs, but it has kept the General Electric report free from all except trifling errors for years.

Considerable effort is expended to make the annual report accurate in another sense: the reporting of problems and difficulties as well as of achievements and triumphs. Opinion research shows that all through the recent troublesome years General Electric's annual report has consistently received high marks from share owners as a credible, reliable document that has avoided a one-sided picture of managerial infallibility.

*An exciting annual report.* For annual reports generally, the presentation of material has tended to follow one of two broad paths: toward a report that puts primary emphasis on impressions of dignity and toward one whose visual impressions aim at color and excitement.

Research conducted for General Electric indicates a demand for both types. One thing many share owners look for in the annual report is reassurance about their investment, and the dignified annual report supplies this by emphasizing formal taste, conservative use of illustrative material and chaste typography set amidst large areas of white space. It speaks of stability, solidity, dependability.

But share owners also like to see signs of forward movement, efforts to generate growth, and management's alertness to new trends and opportunities. The exciting annual report supplies this need by emphasizing modern graphics, dramatic photography, informative headlines rather than mere "category" headlines, journalistic devices to speed communication, and greater informality of presentation throughout. It speaks of a progressive, changing, growth-minded organization.

General Electric favors a report that has color and excitement. The company's emphasis is on progress, on research and development, on developing new products and new markets. General Electric people are on the frontiers of new business developments: atomic power, computers, space satellites; and the company is worldwide in its scope and aspirations.

The use of color photography seems to fit such an enterprise. At least two-thirds of the photographs used in the report are taken on special assignments by the report's editors (the other third comes from operating components, defense agencies, and so on). Leading photographers are assigned, and many man-hours go into setting up photographs, scouting out the best location or vantage point and arranging details with the operating people involved.

The General Electric report is well packed, with too much business at hand to permit much white space. It plunges into the highlights on the inside cover and carries the chairman's message on page 1. It tries to carry this momentum all the way through, using the back cover as an extra picture page. This fullness goes naturally with a diversified company that has a great deal to say to share owners and many deserving activities to discuss. We don't want to burden the share owner with a great bulk of pages—a 36-page annual report is small for a company of our size and diversity—but we hope he agrees that the pages we do print are well filled and hard working.

The report's art consultants are encouraged to reach for design concepts that are appropriate to a progressive company. Expense-creating gimmicks such as gate folds and die-cut covers are not encouraged. But if within the standard letter-size format the artist has ideas for blending pictures, graphs, and typography in a combination that will add to the image of an exciting company, we'll listen.

Research among the company's share owners assures us that this is the kind of report they expect and want from General Electric. Measurements of readership and favorability have risen as the report has moved toward modern journalism and away from financial conservatism.

*Selecting a theme.* The annual report is an impressionistic document, an overview, selective rather than comprehensive. How can it be otherwise when it tries to sum up in a few pages the activities of thousands of people over a year's span? The use of a theme helps in what must be a ruthless winnowing process. The reader of our report may never be aware of a theme at all, although he can usually play back the theme's main points to a researcher. But for those on the transmitting end of this communications process, a theme is almost essential in order to impose order, control, and direction on the chaos of detail.

One type of theme used by many companies is the deliberate playing up of a part of the whole: this year we pay tribute to the sales force, next year the research scientists, and so on. Such a "five year plan" of rotation certainly makes sense in view of the need for selectivity.

However, we have stressed broader themes that apply to the whole company and that enable each annual report to stand by itself. These themes have been appropriate to the results of the year and to the most important of the main currents. In a year of economic downturn, the theme might relate to the efforts of people to minimize the adverse effects and build sales and earnings against the trend (if the year's performance justified such a claim). Special efforts to improve earnings has been the theme in a year when this was clearly the top priority for management. The development of growth businesses aiming at building a "new General Electric" alongside the company's more familiar business lines has been a prominent theme.

Someone has written that the annual report represents the corporation's search for its own identity. A well-chosen theme, growing out of the business rather than being superimposed on it, responsive both to internal emphases and to external changes affecting the business, can help with this quest.

*The unified report.* In one respect, we of General Electric diverge from the practice of most other companies. The idea of a "unified" annual report was developed some years ago in reaction against the trend that was splitting the report into two distinct sections—a "yearbook," or narrative of events and developments, and a financial summary crammed with the year's results in dollars. After having done several reports that seemed schizoid to us, our conclusion was that the practice has a built-in imbalance. It tends to make one part of the report unreadably full of matter and then to wrap this in a glittering promotion piece lacking in significant information.

The practice of a two-phase report also seemed to us to stem from a misreading of the annual report audience. Everyone who produces annual reports worries over the terrific disparities among his readers: the fictitious "Aunt Janes" on the one extreme who will supposedly throw up their hands at anything requiring the least mental effort and, on the other extreme, the security analyst who is a specialist in the industry and will reject any but the most sophisticated concepts. The understandable response: a nice bit of frosting for Aunt Jane and a fruitcake sort of density for the professional, possibly carried to the ultimate in the form of a separately published statistical summary.

Reaction from share owners, however, indicates that whether they fully understand it or not, most share owners do try to read the financial summary and financial statements. Perhaps Aunt Jane will not, but the great majority of readers are not Aunt Janes these days. Many of them feel it is almost a duty to their own investment to at least try to read the real meat of the report. The annual report audience cannot be fairly divided into "serious" and "nonserious" readers.

This idea prompted us to explode the financial section and integrate its main types of information into the principal features of the report. A section on sales would coordinate the figures with information about the year's outstanding shipments and installations. That devoted to earnings would tie together the statistics and the plans of management to reduce costs, increase efficiency, and take other steps to improve the return to share owners. Instead of having a happy essay about employee relations in one place and all the statistics about employee costs and details of benefit plans in another, we would put them together in one complete feature. Instead of a section of pictures on new plants in one spread and all the figures on plant expenditures in the financial section, we would combine the two. With the main subject covered in special sections, the financial summary could be a brief recapping of principal facts plus other financial details not treated more fully elsewhere.

This unified type of report has proved to be a satisfactory development. It paces better the presentation of information and reduces duplication and repetition. It gives depth to results and statistics by relating them to the people and operations that produced them. Research has shown a continued rise in readership by share owners and a greater absorption of the more vital information about General Electric. The best-read features in the report are now most often the ones which are financial in nature.

What about the security analyst? Does he resent having to read virtually all of the annual report rather than a concentrated statistical section? We wondered too; so we gathered several groups of them in roundtable discussions and invited their criticisms. These discussions, and other measurements of security analysts' opinions, establish the fact that the unified annual report fares well with the specialist. Today's analyst has broadened his scope beyond the use of mere accounting and statistical tools. He tries to be as sensitive to *esprit* as to price-earnings ratios. As one senior analyst has written: ". . . our professional requirements are so far-flung in scope, and so demanding in depth of research, that they cannot be met by a single individual. They need teamwork of specialists." For this greatly expanded competence, a broader approach to the annual report is in order both for share owners and investment counselors.

The unified annual report obviously relates to our view of the investor as an individual who takes a many-faceted interest in what is likely to affect his investment. Neither raw figures nor traditional public relations emphases go far enough toward helping him. A responsible welding of the two can, in our estimation, do better for the share owner than either alone.

*The importance of research.* Opinion research has figured prominently in the development of the General Electric annual report during the last decade. The importance of research is that it allows the editors of the annual report to "listen" to share owners, to carry on a kind of dialogue about what interests the reader and what does not. Research sharpens one's understanding of the audience, its characteristics and outlook and, above all, the terrifically subjective attitude it brings to an inspection of the report. As one of our research analysts has put it: "The financial information, for example, is not really seen as a report of a very large business enterprise but rather as a somewhat complicated way of learning 'how my shares are doing.' " Also, research enables the editors to sense areas of potential readership and of possible experimentation—the genesis of new ideas and approaches.

General Electric uses both formal and informal research procedures. The formal surveys, including a large enough sample of share owners to make the extrapolation of results statistically valid, are important to the annual report's editors primarily for the profile they supply of readership patterns. On the basis of past findings, we have made major changes in the report. Features that had come down through the years as inviolate (a whole page for announcements of organization changes, for example) were eliminated when research showed that share owners could not have cared less. Pages that were not doing their job (a highlights page with 17 items) were redesigned (9 items in a larger and better type face), with the result that readership shot up. Use of a short one-page chief executive's message proves out in better readership and more penetrating impressions. Research also testifies to the stopping power of high-quality photographs; for us the evidence is convincing that color pictures pay for themselves in getting the report opened and read by more people. Our unified report grew out of study of research conclusions.

The role of this formal research is exemplified by our experiences in 1962 in changing from distribution in an envelope to a self-mailer.

How would share owners react? Would they notice the change at all? Would there be any objections? Or, as we hoped, would readership improve simply by exposing the share owner directly to the color pictures of the cover? The results are in. The percentage of share owners who "read or looked into" the 1962 annual report jumped ten percentage points over the 1961 report. Not many share owners noticed the change—fewer still had any kind of adverse reaction—but they responded in the way that really counts: by giving us more time and attention than they ever did before.

After a number of years of such research, the seminal effect of each new study naturally begins to thin. Today formal studies are important to us as a continuing check and as an overall measurement of each new report against the trend lines of the past. In a creative sense, more informal types of research now have greater impact. For example, round-table discussions with groups of security analysts and with groups of share owners give us many fresh starting points for creativity. The face-to-face meeting with real people who arrive full of opinions about what has confused them, annoyed them, or bored them is a strong catalyst to creative faculties and a powerful antidote to any tendency to become stuffy or stilted.

One more note needs to be added about share owner research. Wide circulation has been given to a research study which suggests that annual reports are little read and less understood. A good percentage of stockholders are reported, for example, to think a "subsidiary" is a form of financial support dispensed by Government. The picture of business that has been drawn is of groups of men going to immense travail and expense to produce glossy examples of the printer's art which totally fail to communicate. But on examination these conclusions are largely based on questions having to do with *specific knowledge.* On this basis it is always easy to prove that *any* segment of the public is a group of uninformed ninnies. To validate this claim, I have recently run a survey among my associates on the spelling of the name of the Soviet premier. It is a name that all of us have read thousands of times; yet, faced with having to put the letters in the proper order, seven out of ten failed. What this proves about my associates is not that they are illiterate but that they read words rather than letters; they grasp the whole and not necessarily all the parts. (The spelling is Khrushchev.) Against this kind of abuse of research we can stack thick volumes of studies that show that share owners as a whole take the annual report seriously, try to understand it, and do actually come away with the main ideas, whether or not they absorb specific details.

Research keeps us aligned with our audience and provides us with bases for new structures of the imagination. The present editors of General Electric's annual report are so wedded to the use of research that we would feel as though we were flying blind if there were no means of measuring response.

*Keeping a tight rein on costs.* Several years ago our annual report cost over $.30 a copy, including all expenditures for production and distribution except the salaries of the General Electric people working on the report. This seemed fair enough for a report of 32 pages, plus a separate heavy-stock cover printed in full color.

Yet today, without increasing the print run substantially, the unit cost has been lowered to around $.25. This is in spite of increased rates for art work and typesetting, increases in paper prices, and so forth. The trend toward lower costs reflects an increased cost-consciousness all along the line. The editors contribute by holding down such items as photographic costs. To do this, we have become students of the special proclivities of photographers. Assignments that involve hard-to-light scenes such as the whole bay of a factory go to a photographer who is a leader in this type of work. Straight manufacturing shots are done by other photographers, studio shots are assigned to still another specialist, and so on, with a constant effort being made to factor in the photographer's rates with the degree of difficulty the picture entails and its importance to us. We work with international picture agencies who can assign a "local" man whether in Indianapolis or Istanbul, and this saves on travel expenses.

We keep a careful watch on proofs. Beautiful white glossy proofs are nice, but we can read the type on much less costly paper. We try to avoid vendors' overtime charges: before going on overtime, the vendor has to get our approval. Billing terms for designers, artists, and photographers are spelled out in letters of agreement.

A separate production and distribution operation places the printing contract on the basis of competitive bids. Innovations such as that of the change to a self-mailer are worked out by this operation. Before we get into the production schedule, we hold a meeting of the whole team—artists, typesetters, printers, representatives, editors, and the company's own production experts—to guard against any costly hitches later on.

After the report is out, the same group reconvenes and makes a detailed critique of the job just done. Was there any unnecessary slippage? Who caused whom avoidable trouble and expense? What can be done to improve procedures? This brings us back full circle to the plan. In the effort to hold down costs, nothing counts more than getting agreements on main points and principal deadline dates early in the formative stages and then sticking to them. In our annual report work these steps have helped us get more for less.

* * *

So much for our working philosophy. Long as it is, this summation does not touch on many questions that the annual report editor must try to decide: how much direct promotion of products to allow in a report; whether to use annual report space to run an "editorial"—to argue a cause; how to schedule other work so that at peak times one's whole attention can be given to the annual report; how to achieve a dignity of style without slipping over into stuffiness and pomposity; how to satisfy managers' desires to put our best foot forward without having share owners regard the effort as merely a sales pitch or commercial.

This chapter has obviously discussed the annual report from the viewpoint of the editor as distinct from that of the manager, but it can be argued that the editor's viewpoint is valid in a book for management. By developing a better understanding of how the editor must regard this critical and difficult publication, the manager can become a more effective supervisor of and contributor to the report's evolution. No editor will object to the assertion that an informed, interested, and constructive management is a prime requisite for a successful annual report.

# THE POST-MEETING REPORT •

**FRANKLIN MOORE**

*and*

**GALE D. WALLACE**

---

THE PHILOSOPHY OF THE MANAGEMENT of United Fruit Company is to keep its thousands of shareholders constantly informed on the activities and progress of the company. Inherent in this philosophy is the belief that shareholders should be informed factually and promptly on all significant happenings. To this end, the post-annual-meeting report is an integral part of its total shareholder communications program. The word "total" is used advisedly because we regard all of our shareholder communications as comprising a comprehensive program—one part of which is the post-meeting report. We publish the annual report and send quarterly letters to shareholders and special letters covering major occurrences taking place between the regular reports already mentioned. In addition, each and every shareholder who writes to the company receives a prompt and to-the-point reply. All of this is supplemented by many telephone calls and personal visits by our owners. Countless hours are spent by our financial people discussing the company with representatives of institutional accounts and investment houses. Thus we believe that no one medium of communications standing by itself can successfully maintain proper shareholder relations.

Since the company's annual meeting takes place approximately three and one-half months after the close of the fiscal year, the meeting offers an ideal opportunity to update the annual report by indicating the progress and problems which may have arisen in the meantime. The reporting of the proceedings of the meeting in the post-meeting report provides a permanent record of the meeting and, in addition, permits us to brief all those shareholders who were unable to attend the meeting. Although a large percentage of outstanding stock is represented at our annual

---

FRANKLIN MOORE is Secretary and GALE D. WALLACE is Associate Director of Public Relations, United Fruit Company, Boston, Massachusetts.

meetings, we realize that only a small number of our owners can appear in person. The post-meeting report is tailored especially to those unable to attend.

In recent years, the post-meeting report has become an increasingly popular and useful tool for those responsible for shareholder and public relations. In the not-too-distant past, many annual meetings of large companies were held in relatively inconvenient and inaccessible locations, were poorly attended, and were very briefly reported in the press. Quite frequently the companies themselves gave only passing reference to the annual meeting in some shareholder communication issued primarily for another purpose. The change in attitude of today's managements toward post-meeting reports seems to correspond to the changes which led to the holding of annual meetings in more accessible locations. Some companies have even gone to the extent of rotating the meetings from place to place or holding regional meetings with the objective of encouraging active participation by maximum numbers of the owners of the corporations.

Companies presently have vastly different ideas as to how full a report should be issued with respect to the proceedings of the annual meeting. Some are relatively brief, mentioning only the official action taken, with short references to speeches made and questions asked. The management of the United Fruit Company feels that in view of the fact that the annual meeting is generally the only time during the year when a face-to-face public exchange of views takes place between the management and the owners of the business, this event is worth recounting in a rather extensive fashion for the benefit of shareholders who are unable to attend the meeting, as well as for interested members of the financial community and the general public. In accomplishing this purpose, we simplify and omit to the extent possible the legalistic, parliamentary portions of the proceedings but otherwise edit only repetitive remarks and items judged to be not of general importance or interest. Speeches made by management are reported in full. It is our feeling that the annual meeting and, consequently, the post-meeting report present opportunities to "sell" the company and to project the company's image in the best possible light to a selected segment of the general public having special importance to the management.

Planning for the issuance of the post-meeting report coincides with that for the annual meeting and is participated in by both the public relations department and the secretary's office, together with a small committee. At this point it is appropriate to note that our shareholder relations program requires and receives maximum coordination among the public relations department, the secretary's office, and the treasurer—the latter being responsible primarily for dealing with the investment community which, as is the case with most other publicly owned companies, represents an appreciable percentage of United Fruit stock. Constant discussions among these three departments of the company assure us that we are addressing our program to the desires of our shareholders.

If an extensive post-meeting report is to be made, it is necessary to have an accurate and complete running account of what is said and done by any and all participants in the meeting. To this end, a stenotype transcript is taken. Experience has shown us that the stenotypist requires some assistance, best provided by a company employee familiar with executives and who is available to move about and ask the necessary questions in order to properly identify participants in the meeting. As a double check, a tape recording of the proceedings is also made. This may seem to be unnecessary, but we have found that such a tape is a valuable adjunct to the stenotype record in avoiding errors in recounting the proceedings, and the cost of the taping is extremely modest.

It has been our observation that post-meeting reports are too often not particularly interesting from a visual standpoint and sometimes give the appearance of being rather formidable documents. It is our thought that carefully selected photographs not only dress up the report but lend interest. It has been said on fairly good authority that two of the principal reasons that shareholders attend annual meetings are to take a look at the board of directors and to hear the president's address. In view of this, we feel it is a good idea to include the president's address and a scattering of photographs of directors, as well as those of other company officials and shareholders participating. Lighting in most meeting places usually leaves something to be desired—either it is too dim or not uniformly bright enough. Speakers, being intent on their remarks, do not always photograph to the best advantage. Back lighting throws the face in a shadow with strange optical effects that may render the individual unrecognizable even to his best friends. We attempt to avoid these many pitfalls by having two photographers, shooting at different speeds, circulating as unobtrusively as possible during the meeting. The photographers are assigned assistants to aid in shooting and identification.

The determination of the cover illustration for the post-meeting report is normally one of the last decisions made. In many cases a photograph taken before, after, or during the course of the meeting, involving a shareholder or a group of shareholders together with company officials, tells a suitable story. Just in case such a photograph does not materialize, a designed cover is always held in readiness.

The question as to whether shareholders who pose questions should be identified or merely designated as "a shareholder" is of a controversial nature. It is the feeling of our management that since management representatives are always identified in the post-meeting report, there is no justification for not identifying the shareholder.

Sizes of post-meeting reports vary—from those that will fit into a standard business envelope to those of approximately letter size. Our company used the small size for several years but found that it was not well adapted to full reporting and particularly limited the use of photographs. On the theory that numerous shareholders preserve in their files the annual reports and other communications of the company, it was felt that it might be more convenient to issue the post-meeting report in a page size approximating that of the annual report, and this was done in 1963 with, we feel, considerable success. And we have considerably more freedom with respect to photographs by using the larger size. The increase in the page size of the report does not appear to have added significantly to the cost except for the fact that more photographs than usual were included.

There appears to be an increasing trend on the part of corporate managements to bulk-mail annual reports, post-meeting reports, and similar material. For the past two years, the United Fruit Company's post-meeting report has been a self-mailer. Prior to the printing, the local post office is checked to determine what regulations, if any, make necessary a change in the format or plan for distribution. All post-meeting reports distributed within the United States are bulk-mailed, thereby saving on envelopes and taking advantage of the bulk rate, which is considerably cheaper than either first- or third-class mailings. Our experience is that in most cases reports are received by the shareholders in good condition, although bulk-mail distribution is admittedly somewhat slower in some areas than other classes of mail. Foreign mailings necessarily must be either first class or airmail, or, alternatively, air-expressed in lots for local distribution.

Now having gone to all the work, expense, and trouble of producing the post-meeting report, the logical question is, "What is the shareholder or general-public reaction to such a report?" As those concerned with shareholder relations know only too well, any time a corporation having many thousands of shareholders issues a statement or a release individually—no matter how innocuous—there is always some reaction: sometimes faint, sometimes violent. This depends primarily upon the content of the communication, as does the volume of comments. So far as the United Fruit Company's post-meeting report is concerned, the record shows that most of the communications have been complimentary, containing such expressions as "superb," "most complete and informative," "interesting and informative," "excellent report—read twice." There are always one or two comments expressing the thought that if the post-meeting report were eliminated, the dividend could be increased, and a few isolated comments criticizing in some respect an action of the management as recounted in the report. Perhaps the most gratifying correspondence originates from those requesting additional information based on the proceedings or raising further questions concerning some of the matters discussed at the meeting.

The United Fruit Company has never conducted a formal survey among shareholders to determine the extent of readership of the post-meeting report; but based on our direct contacts with the owners and the constant follow-up by public relations, and our secretary and treasurer, we do feel that a sufficiently large segment of the shareholders and the financial community does read our report so that there is no question as to the justification of issuing it.

# REACHING STOCKHOLDERS THROUGH INVESTOR PUBLICATIONS •

STANLEY SAUERHAFT

THE MANAGEMENTS OF PUBLICLY OWNED COMPANIES are required to keep their stockholders reasonably informed on the financial status of the business. The Securities and Exchange Commission and the various stock exchanges have regulations stipulating certain minimum communications. But more and more these days, progressive corporate managements are coming to realize that there is great potential strength in their stockholder families, and through their public relations advisors they have been developing ways of tapping this strength and enhancing its usefulness to the company.

The stockholders of a company are predisposed toward that company. After all, they have invested their funds to buy a portion of the company. If this sense of ownership can be further stimulated, these thousands of stockholders can be converted into customers for the company's products, salesmen for its stock and products, and advocates of its position in times of difficulty.

Because most publicly owned companies have thousands of stockholders spread throughout the United States and often abroad, it is virtually impossible for management to communicate in person with more than a small fraction of the company's owners. The job of reaching the entire stockholder family must be done through the printed word.

---

STANLEY SAUERHAFT is President, Howard Chase Associates, Inc., New York, New York.

Unquestionably the most important single tool of management communications with stockholders is the annual report. For many years corporate managements issued yearly reports that fulfilled only the bare legal requirements of audited income statements, balance sheets, and notice of the coming annual meeting. Modern annual reports have letters from the chief executive; extensive reviews of the past year's operations; charts and graphs to clarify trends of sales, earnings, dividends, and capital expenditures; black-and-white as well as color pictures; and simplified explanations of complex financial data. Management realizes that the average stockholder is financially unsophisticated and easily confused by a profit and loss statement. In order to get the report noted and understood, the company must make it attractive and easy and interesting to read.

But to maintain rapport with any group, communication must be more often than once a year. To be truly effective, it must be continuous, for the essence of education is frequency of exposure—repetition of impact, as advertising men put it. Also the stockholder family itself is continually changing. Some stockholders sell out their shares while new ones come into the fold. It is not uncommon for a listed company to have a 20 per cent turnover of stockholders during the course of a year.

Furthermore, the annual report is a very large dose of financial communications dished out all at once. For most stockholders it is far too much for them to digest fully; only a portion is likely to be absorbed. This is particularly true because of the fairly inflexible timing of most company annual reports. Because they are on a January-to-December fiscal year, audited financial statements are usually not available until some time in February. Thus the complete annual report is finally printed and put into the mails in March. Stockholders who own shares in several companies often find their mails bulging during a two-week period in mid-March with the reports of all their companies. In addition to the usual competition of magazines, television, newspapers, and sundry other printed media, these carefully—even lovingly—prepared reports have to compete with each other for the stockholder's narrow span of attention. Small wonder that even the best of reports has only a limited impact on stockholders.

Some companies, aware that the timing of the annual report mailing weakens its impact, have developed a "flash" report that is mailed shortly after the first of the new year. This digest of the upcoming full report has the dual advantage of arriving when the past year is still fairly fresh in mind and well ahead of the deluge of competing company communications.

The flash report has still another major edge. It does not have to compete with the annual figures of hundreds of other companies for the attention of the financial press. The traditional mid-March period finds the press inundated with thousands of annual reports and news releases based on the information therein. Only a few companies can be given adequate attention in the limited columns of the financial papers, whereas in mid-January, when the limited number of flash annual reports arrive, the competition for the column inches is far less keen. Consequently, the important annual figures can be given better treatment, more stockholders can read about their company in the press (with concomitant feelings of pride), and more potential investors can learn of the results of the company's previous year's activities. The Chesapeake and Ohio Railroad has used the technique of the flash report most effectively for a number of years.

One of the most commonly used techniques of reaching investors between annual reports is the interim report. Some companies issue semi-annual reports, but most of the larger listed companies now regularly publish quarterly reports. Several years ago Corn Products Company, one of the more progressive companies in the field of stockholder communications, decided to convert its quarterly report into a pocket-sized magazine. In addition to the usual quarterly balance sheet, it expanded the interpretive letter to stockholders from the chief executive and added a feature section of general corporate news plus one in-depth treatment of some facet of the company's business each quarter. The publication was named *Spotlight.*

One quarter the "spotlight" was on Corn Products' educational program; another quarter it was on a new chief executive; still another was on its international division. Its biggest domestic plant, a new television advertising program, an anecdotal biography of several of its major consumer brands were some other featured segments in the quarterly *Spotlight.* Over a period of years this has served to acquaint Corn Products' stockholders better with the people, plants, products, and personnel of the company they own. It has also been quite helpful to security analysts, according to comments recorded in the course of several opinion surveys.

Another opportunity to reach stockholders regularly is afforded by the quarterly mailing of the dividend check. Often these checks do not coincide with the dates of quarterly reports but require a separate mailing. This additional mailing may carry a "hitchhiker" in the form of a sheet or sheets the same size as the dividend check. These envelope stuffers may be reduced-price product coupons for stockholder sampling, new product announcements, reproductions of national magazine advertisements, or announcements of new executive changes. This technique enables the company to add four more contacts each year with the stockholders at no additional postage cost.

One of the key objectives of an investor relations program is to create a sense of personal identification with the company on the part of the shareholders. It is good tactics for management to try to humanize the company because people can relate to other people much more easily than they can to inanimate objects. This seems so obvious, but it is surprising how many corporate managements ignore this simple principle.

A good way to start off the management-stockholder relationship is with a welcoming letter from the president to the new stockholder as soon as the registration of the shares is accomplished. This letter should be accompanied by a copy of the company's latest annual report as well as the most recent interim report. Here is a sample of the letter that is sent by the management of Corn Products Company to its new stockholders:

> Fellow Shareholder:
>
> Thank you for placing your confidence in Corn Products. We believe you will share our enthusiasm for the company's future—its prospects for continued leadership, growth, and profitability.
>
> You own much more than just a stock certificate. You are now an owner of a diversified enterprise providing useful products for the home, industry, and the farm. You own a share of a worldwide company, strong on research and receptive to new ideas. You are entitled to a voice in the business and we hope you let us have the benefit of your opinions without hesitancy. We say this because it is our conviction that management operates most effectively when it has the support of owners who are well informed and highly interested in the company's progress.
>
> It is the goal of Corn Products' management to provide maximum security for your investment . . . to promote sound business growth so that your holdings may increase in value . . . and to provide a satisfactory return in the form of dividends. It is, by the way, the policy of the Board of Directors to consider dividend action quarterly. Corn Products has paid its quarterly dividend regularly since 1919.
>
> We are proud of our people, plants, and products and hope you will become better acquainted with them. We believe the enclosed literature will provide you with further understanding of the nature and extent of our operations.
>
> If, at any time, you would like more information on any aspect of our business, we will do our best to provide it. We look forward to a long and pleasant association with you.

May we also direct your attention to the enclosed U.S. Treasury Department Form 3435. Your prompt cooperation in providing the information required will be greatly appreciated.

Sincerely,

(signature)

President

Corn Products also sends along to the new share owner a copy of a publication called *Almanac,* a compendium of facts about the company. The booklet, which is revised every six months, is also sent to security analysts, financial reporters, and other interested persons wanting a quick reference to all aspects of this international company. Included in *Almanac* are some brief historical data and significant chronology of events since the company's founding: such vital statistics as the number of employees throughout the world, the number of shareholders and their geographical distribution, and raw materials used by the company; a brief description of its products; a listing and description of its directors and corporate officers; a ten-year comparative table of financial highlights, such as domestic and international sales and earnings, the percentage of net income to net sales, working capital, and capital expenditures; a ten-year comparative table of common share data, such as shares outstanding, domestic and international earnings per share, dividends per share, and book value; a breakdown of the company's capital structure; the distribution of its worldwide sales dollar; a listing of each company plant in the United States and abroad with its address and plant manager; a description of each major division with its chief officer; and a listing of the company's advertising agencies, public relations firm, auditor, transfer agents, registrars, and stock exchange memberships.

The warm letter of welcome to the company's stockholder family, along with all the pertinent information about the company and its operations, serves to show the new investor that the management of this company cares about him and desires his real and active interest in the affairs of the company. The new relationship is off to a good start.

Good stockholder relationships develop two-way communications between corporate management and the investor. When the investor writes to the company, he gets a prompt and courteous reply. He knows the company is interested in his point of view. When the company wants to convey its position on some new Federal legislation, it knows it will receive a sympathetic and attentive hearing by the stockholder.

This relationship is terminated when the stockholder sells his shares. Some managements have adopted the practice of sending letters of regret upon learning that the stockholder has sold his shares. The purpose of such letters is to learn why the investor decided to sell. Sometimes a pattern of reasons for selling may be discerned from a number of answers to these letters of regret. But the subject is a very sensitive one. Note how carefully it is handled in the following example by one of the most experienced of all companies in the area of investor relations, The Borden Company:

> Dear . . . . . :
>
> You are no longer listed as a stockholder of The Borden Company. This does not necessarily mean that you have sold your stock. You may have transferred your shares to the name of a broker or some other person. But if you have disposed of your stock, I would like to know your reasons—unless they are personal.
>
> I am not trying to influence any decision on investments. I would like to know, however, if company policies or activities affected your decision. Did we keep you informed about Borden's? I shall appreciate a frank reply.
>
> If you have sold stock but would like to receive our next Annual Report, please let me know. I shall be happy to send it to you.
>
> Cordially yours,
>
> (signature)
>
> President
>
> P.S. I hope that you will continue to buy Borden's products and to ask your dealers to stock them.

Most of the communications we have discussed thus far have been designed to stimulate the stockholders' sense of partnership in the company by informing them of the various facets of the company and attempting to interest them in the operations and products of the company and thus engage their sympathetic and active support. Corporate management also wants to stimulate the stockholders' sense of pride in the company and reinforce their conviction that their investment is wise and sound. Management hopes the reported operating results will achieve this. But there are certain things that management in all good taste cannot say about its stewardship of the business, although it would dearly like them to be said to their stockholders.

Occasionally an opportunity arises to get this kind of message across. A brokerage house may have prepared a very detailed factual account of the company's operations with some comment on its prospects for the future. A business magazine, like *Fortune* or *Business Week,* may have done a major article on the company with favorable comment on the quality of the management and its conduct of the business. A reprint of the brokerage report or magazine article can be sent to each stockholder with a short, friendly note from the president of the company commending it to the stockholder for its interesting point of view and assessment of the company's capabilities. This third-party endorsement, especially when it is by a prestige Wall Street house or financial publication, can be very effective.

Other periodic mailings that tend to enlarge the stockholders' fund of information about the company, while at the same time serving to enhance their opinion of the company, include: copies of speeches made by company officials before societies of security analysts, copies of company publications such as dealer bulletins and employee magazines that have articles of particular interest to stockholders, statements of principal executives before legislative committee hearings, advance copies of advertisements of a new product line about to break in national magazines and newspapers throughout the country. The latter has the additional value of making the stockholders feel they are privileged to learn important company plans before the general public learns of them—a fringe benefit of ownership. The chances are also quite good that many of those stockholders will be among the first to buy the product.

In the case of "glamour products" such as automobiles and TV receivers, some companies make it a practice to invite stockholders in key areas to dealer preview showings in advance of public introduction. Pictures taken at such affairs can often form the basis of interesting mailings to the stockholder family.

How does management know to whom it is speaking in its publications? What are the company's stockholders like? How old are they? Where do they live? Why did they buy the company's stock? Are they likely to buy more stock or sell it soon? Do they own stock in other companies? What do they think of the way the company is being run? Are they buying the company's products?

The answers to some of these questions can be supplied by the company's transfer agent, who can draw up a chart of stock ownership by states, average number of shares held, average length of time held, and so forth. But the most important questions can only be answered by an opinion survey. A few corporations employ opinion research firms to interview selected stockholders and to compile the results. Others utilize mail survey techniques built around direct questionnaires to all the company's stockholders. The latter, in addition to being generally less expensive, has the additional value of impressing stockholders with management's interest in them. The results of these surveys can be valuable guides to management in communicating more effectively with its share owner family.

We have not discussed here the special publications—mostly bulletins and letters—which proliferate at the time of a proxy fight. That is an abnormal situation. We have confined ourselves to the more normal considerations that face most members of management: how best to fulfill the responsibility to the owners of the business and at the same time to derive the maximum advantage for the company from its body of stockholders.

# SECTION IV

---

## *Professional Investor Relations*

*If a company restricts its concern to share owners of record, it is doing only half the job of investor relations. The institutional investors require at least equal attention: banks, brokers, foundations, insurance and investment companies, mutual funds, and pension funds. Those in advisory positions to these professional investors—the financial analysts—require specialized attention. They gather information from company reports, visits to the company, conferences, and special events.*

# A LOOK AT PROFESSIONAL INVESTOR RELATIONS •

ROBERT R. AUGSBURGER

How many of us have ever examined the process by which individual stockholders obtain information and make investment decisions concerning our companies? Do they come directly to us for information on the effect of a proposed acquisition, for an explanation of dividend policy, for an opinion on management's capabilities, or for an estimate of future earnings? Probably not. Whom, then, do they turn to?

They consult with an investment officer in a bank trust department; they talk with stockbrokers; they read the *Wall Street Journal,* the financial section of their local newspaper, and other financial publications; they subscribe to one or more investment advisory services. Members of the professional investment community are the source of the facts and the opinions which will lead to stockholder decisions in regard to the securities of the company. And this process is repeated daily by many of the 17 million stockholders in this country.

Responsible executives should ask how well the company is fulfilling its responsibility to the stockholders by keeping these opinion leaders adequately informed of company affairs. Does it ignore them? Does it merely tolerate them? Or does it carefully cultivate them? I believe that professional investors should be cultivated. As a general background for subsequent chapters on this subject, we are going to determine who these people are; the opportunities and problems in communicating with them;

---

Robert R. Augsburger is Vice President, Donaldson, Lufkin & Jenrette, Inc., New York, New York.

and, last but not least, the value to the company in developing good relations with the professional investment community.

### A BREAKDOWN ON PROFESSIONAL INVESTORS

In its simplest form, the professional investment community can be broken down into three groups: distributors of securities, buyers of securities, and advisers to the professional and individual investor. While there is often an overlapping of functions of these three groups, we shall treat them as separate and distinct.

In the selling, marketing, or distributing group, we find the investment banker and the broker-dealer. They represent firms which range from the large, highly organized national distributors of securities—such as First Boston Corporation and Merrill Lynch, Pierce, Fenner & Smith—to the small, local firms found in almost every city across the country.

Just as these firms differ materially in size, they also differ significantly in approach, objectives, and type of customer. Generally, the type of customer the firm seeks to cultivate determines the approach taken by its representatives. The distinctions among them are not all black and white. However, in planning and conducting an investor relations program, it is well to recognize the distinctions and the reasons for them.

A national firm which caters primarily to individual investors must be prepared to provide information on a wide variety of industries and individual companies. Note the use of the word "information." Because of the pressures of time and the number of securities followed, these people seldom have the opportunity for detailed analysis, nor are their clients basically interested in such analysis.

The local firm which concentrates on individuals will tend to specialize in the securities of companies located in its area. Here it has the opportunity to get to know the managements and to discover which companies have investment potential. In addition, it will probably draw upon a New York correspondent firm for information and analysis of securities traded on national markets.

In the major financial centers, we have a third type of distributor firm—the one which specializes in institutional investors and wealthy individuals. Here the caliber of information and analysis is considerably more sophisticated. Fewer companies are followed with regularity: some firms will follow only the very large or "blue chip" companies or a particular industry or group of industries. Others will concentrate in depth on smaller companies or new industries. And still others will attempt to provide a cross section of both. The approach taken by representatives of these firms appears to be considerably more professional, and indeed it is, because their customers demand it. The buying power and the needs of these customers permit a more thorough use of time and talent.

The second group in the professional investment community is made up of buyers of securities. These are the individuals who are paid to manage the investments of institutions—mutual funds, life and casualty insurance companies, pension funds, bank trust departments, college endowment funds, and so forth.

These people have become an increasingly important source of capital. During the past 30 years we have witnessed the institutionalization of our bond market. Today, with only a few minor exceptions, the institutions these buyers manage represent the only source of long-term funds available through the debt route. At the rate assets of institutions are growing, we may well see a greater institutionalization of the equity market. Let us consider the following facts:

- In 1950 there were 13,000 private pension and profit sharing plans having assets of $11.6 billion. In 1963 there were over 65,000 plans with total assets in excess of $61 billion. New money each year now amounts to over $3.5 billion.
- The percentage of the private pension funds invested in equities has increased—from 27 per cent in 1955 to more than 45 per cent in 1962.
- During this same period, state and municipal pension funds grew from $5.3 to $24.3 billion. New money each year amounts to about $2.5 billion. Most of these funds are now invested in governments and high-grade corporate bonds, but they are gradually swinging over to mortgages, lease backs, and—in some cases—common stocks.
- The assets of open- and closed-end investment companies have been growing at an annual compound rate of approximately 20 per cent. At the end of 1962, their total assets were estimated to be close to $24.5 billion. By far the largest percentage of their assets is invested in common stocks.
- Insurance company assets have grown at a 5.3 per cent rate and now exceed $160 billion. Net new money each year amounts to over $7 billion.
- At the end of 1962, the holdings by institutional investors of only the stocks listed on the New York Stock Exchange amounted to $65 billion, or 19 per cent of the total value of New York Stock Exchange stocks.

These are formidable figures, and they point out the growing financial power placed in the hands of the investment managers of these funds.

The third group within the professional investment community is the investment advisors and counselors. Like the brokerage group, these people do not make ultimate investment decisions. Their function is to screen, recommend, and follow individual securities for both individual and institutional clients. Representation in this group ranges from the well-known advisory publications to the large, sophisticated investment counseling firms. In addition, many mutual fund management companies and large brokerage firms operate investment advisory departments as separate functions of their businesses.

Within the framework of this investment community, we have a myriad of individuals—partners, investment officers, portfolio managers, security analysts, market analysts, registered representatives, market letter writers, traders, proxy clerks, and many others.

The man with whom we are primarily concerned is the security analyst. Most of the information and opinions about a company, which are circulated in the investment community itself and the investing public at large, originate with this man. While he does not make investment decisions himself, he has a great deal of influence upon those who do.

While generalizations can be dangerous, we can categorize analysts into four major groups:

1. Those working for a major trust company, mutual fund, pension fund, or insurance company. Because these men are directly associated with the ultimate investment decision, where sizable sums of other people's money are involved, they have the greatest degree of responsibility. The performance of the institution's portfolio is in large part dependent upon the reliability of their information and their evaluation of management. While primarily concerned with long-term trends, these men must still be alert to current internal and external developments. Information given them is seldom disseminated outside their own organizations.
2. The second group is represented by the analyst working for the large investment counseling firm or institutional brokerage firm. Although not involved in the final investment decision, this man is still a working partner of the institutional analyst; and the approach taken is much the same. Quite frequently he is called upon by his clients to initiate and maintain contact with company managements. The investment policies and objectives of his clients often dictate his areas of interest. He is relied upon not only for follow-up but also as a principal source of new investment ideas. The information received from management is generally distributed to selected clients in periodic basic or interim memoranda.

3. The third group is made up of analysts or, possibly, portfolio managers with the smaller mutual funds, insurance companies, and trust companies. The size of their portfolios is insufficient to justify the thoroughness demanded by the larger institutions. They generally rely completely on investment counsel and institutional brokers for management contact and company information.
4. The final group is composed of those analysts working for brokerage firms and investment advisory services whose customers are primarily individuals. Most of the small investors in the United States are clients of these firms. Because their customers' interests are widely varied, ranging from the rankest speculation to the bluest "blue chip," these men must follow literally hundreds of companies. And they are frequently pressed into finding companies and writing reports as "merchandise" for the firm's sales force to sell. Many of these men are very capable; however, the pressures of time prevent them from being as thorough as some others, and they often give the impression to company officials of being superficial. This does not necessarily mean that the analyst is not doing a good job: he is simply doing all he is able to do. Because these people represent one of the main communication links to the investing public, it is most important for a company to see that they have the facts straight.

## THE MANAGEMENT OF PROFESSIONAL INVESTOR RELATIONS

We have in professional investor relations a new and growing area of financial management. It is an area where a company can just let things happen, willy-nilly, or it can *make* things happen. One of the major management functions is control, and I believe that control is just as applicable to investor relations as it is to costs, personnel, cash, or any other business factor. There are a number of ways to approach it.

First, we must establish an objective. I can think of no better one than that of the General Electric Company: "To provide better, more accurate information to security analysts so that over a period of time they will tend to base their appraisals of the company's securities more upon the available factual and real information about the company and less upon rumor, speculation, and hunch. . . ."

Second, we should make an honest appraisal of our company's investment potential. Most managements would like to consider their company as a growth company. But let's be realistic: many are in highly cyclical or competitive businesses where year-to-year growth is hard to come by.

If they want to have good, long-term investor relations, my advice is: "Don't try to present yourself as something that you aren't." There are still a lot of investors, both individual and institutional, who look upon stability of earnings and dividends as an investment virtue.

Third, we should appoint one person as the principal contact for security analysts. In a small company, this will probably be the president. In the medium-size to larger company, it will probably be the vice president of finance or the treasurer. In many large companies and occasionally in smaller ones, the demands upon top executive time by analysts are so great that it may be desirable to give this responsibility to a staff person. Who that man is or where he fits into the organizational structure is not particularly important. What is important is that he have the confidence of management, the authority to speak for the company, access to information about the entire company, and good judgment. It may take longer for this man to gain the confidence of analysts and to get across that he is properly informed, but most analysts often discover that such a man is in a better position to serve their needs than top corporate officers.

Fourth, we must decide what and how much information we are going to give out to analysts. Many managements limit information on the grounds that it might be competitively harmful to their business. In these cases, the analyst can often go across the street to competitors and find out exactly what he wants to know. Emphasis should be placed upon increasing the amount of information made available to analysts and stockholders.

There are a number of critical information areas on which a policy decision should be made. Among them are the following:

1. *Sales and earnings forecasts.* Some companies follow a policy that under no circumstances are sales and earnings forecasts given to analysts and that giving out forecasts can create nightmares. However, a reasonable range of probabilities of sales and earnings is given by some companies for the *current* year. After all, earnings are the essence of market valuation. Long-term economic trends should be reviewed to permit the analyst to follow current developments in their longer-term context.
2. *Actual sales and earnings.* Under no circumstances should actual monthly, quarterly, or annual sales and earnings be given to analysts unless and *until* they are released to the general public. These data are in the category of "inside" information, and all too many companies treat this matter much too lightly.
3. *Dividend policy.* This is a touchy and difficult subject, but one that is also critical to market appraisal. The board of directors should

adopt a policy and make it known to the investing public. We can then explain to the analyst the various factors which might cause a future change in that policy.

4. *Sales and profits by division or product group.* This information is certainly pertinent to an evaluation of profit potential and profit risks. Here competitive aspects weigh heavily in determining what should be given out. Some companies give approximations to keep the analyst in the ballpark.
5. *Merger considerations.* Company policy can be broadly outlined. However, negotiations or completion should be held in confidence until publicly announced as this again falls in the category of "inside" information.
6. *Financing plans.* Certainly the need for financing or the circumstances under which it might be needed should be discussed. There is some question on specific form and timing. However, elevator operators, waiters, and similar "members" of the investment community have ears; it is best to get this subject out into the open.
7. *New product development.* The ire of the Securities and Exchange Commission has already been aroused by "sneak previews" for analysts of new product developments. If it has significant potential, no one should get advance official information prior to public announcement. In any event, the sales and earnings potential of any new product should be discussed with analysts to make sure they don't get it out of context.

Whatever we decide to tell analysts, we must be sure of one thing—always being honest and straightforward about the problem or negative areas as well as the positive aspects. There is nothing that will hurt a company in the investment community for a longer period of time than a reputation for being misleading and untrustworthy: the word does get around.

The next step is to determine the audience. Who is in it? Certainly not merely the 8,500 or more members of the Financial Analysts Federation. In terms of an awareness and general knowledge of the company, the audience could be as large as 500 to 1,000 analysts. There are three means of communicating with them:

1. Regular stockholder publications—annual reports, quarterly reports, and so on.
2. A special handbook for analysts, giving detailed background on company policies, objectives, and operations. This can save time we might otherwise spend in covering general details in a personal interview.

3. Appearances by management representatives at the regular meetings held among the 35 local societies in the Financial Analysts Federation.

In terms of specific, detailed knowledge of the company, the audience may range from 10 to 100 analysts—the number probably dependent upon the size of the company. In addition to the use of stockholder reports and analyst-society meetings, specialists and others who have a deeper interest in the company can be reached by:

1. Encouraging them to visit company offices at regular intervals. This gives them the opportunity to meet various members of top management over a period of time.
2. Initiating periodic contacts with them in their own offices. This saves them time and gives them the opportunity to be up to date on current activities.
3. Special meetings with management personnel. An occasional luncheon or dinner meeting with a small group of analysts provides the opportunity for informal discussion and appraisal of management.
4. Plant tours, where applicable, give them a chance to meet middle management, appraise organization and housekeeping, and get more detailed background on the business.
5. Perhaps even the issuance of a periodic, interpretative newsletter would be desirable.

## THE VALUES TO BE GAINED

Now that all is said and done, we need to know just what the value of a professional investor relations program is for a company. The benefits can be stated as follows:

- It signifies that we are doing our best to make sure that the market price of our stock is based upon fact and is a fair one for both buyer and seller. There will never be a more dissatisfied person than the one who has bought at a high price or sold at a low price created by rumor or misinformation.
- It provides a second and important line of communication between the company and its present stockholders.
- It provides virtually the only means of reaching potential new stockholders. Remember it takes a buyer for every seller. Only by creating a group of knowledgeable potential buyers can we count on having good marketability and a fair pricing of our securities.
- It creates a recognition and knowledge of our company which is

essential to obtaining the best possible terms on new-money financing or acquistion financing.

- It establishes helpful contacts in setting up private financing whether debt, equity, sale-leaseback, or other.
- It provides a helpful playback or sounding board on evaluating management policies which directly affect stockholders, such as dividend policy, compensation programs, return on investment, and so on.
- It can provide support for management in proxy solicitations.

Analysts, the investment community, and stockholders are here to stay. If we ignore them, they will ignore us. In terms of mutual interest, the businessman's closest ally is the investing public. Unless we treat it honestly and fairly, we will have no other means of political or economic support.

# THE FINANCIAL ANALYST'S PROFESSION •

WILLIAM C. NORBY

THE STATISTICIAN IN THE BACK ROOM of the brokerage office of 35 years ago has become the professional financial analyst of today. The Financial Analysts Federation is his professional organization, and it has over 8,250 members in the United States and Canada. Across the seas, he finds kindred organizations in Europe, Australia, and Japan growing rapidly in membership. The stature of the financial analyst is well established and his horizon is continually expanding. Anyone interested in or responsible for a program of investor relations should know the analyst and his professional organization.

## THE PROFESSIONAL FINANCIAL ANALYST

The term "professional" is employed in a wide variety of contexts and meanings in the investment world and in business generally. As used to describe analysts and their activities, it connotes specialized knowledge and intensive preparation in the field of finance and investments coupled with high ethical standards in the investigation and dissemination of reports, analyses, and recommendations. A set of analytical principles has been developed to identify further the field, but they are not yet so clearly defined as are accounting principles, for example. A professional degree, "Chartered Financial Analyst," has been created to indicate mastery of this body of knowledge and set of principles, based on successful completion of a series of examinations. Financial analysis has become a truly professional field.

Despite the unifying aspects of professionalism, analysts are a heterogeneous group described in a variety of ways. The broadest term is "financial analyst," but as generally employed it is not meant to include

WILLIAM C. NORBY is Vice President, Harris Trust & Savings Bank, Chicago, Illinois, and President of The Financial Analysts Federation.

corporate financial analysis carried on by the financial vice president or the comptroller. An alternative term is "securities analyst," which is accurate but more limited than the term "investment analyst." This latter term is my personal preference since it encompasses the whole field of the investment of capital, of which securities are a primary medium, and it includes not only the individual securities—stocks or bonds—but also the portfolio of securities. But "financial analyst" has become the generally accepted term, and so it will be employed henceforth in this chapter.

Financial analysts represent a wide range of interests which can be classified basically as "buying" or "selling." On the "buying" side, analysts are employed by such institutions as bank trust departments, insurance companies, foundations, pension funds, and investment companies to research and select individual securities for purchase or sale and to participate in portfolio management. On the "selling" side, analysts are employed by securities dealers to prepare investment reports and recommendations for purchase and sale and for distribution to customers—both institutional and individual. Many analysts in both categories specialize in a particular industry and become notable experts in the technical and operating phases as well as the financial factors of these industries. Interspersed among these main groups are many contributory and allied activities such as those of analytical firms which provide services to both buyers and sellers, teachers of business and finance, and economists.

Fundamentally, analysts seek the same answers in the same way regardless of the economic interests they represent. Collectively, they can have an important influence on the market for a security because their recommendations direct the flow of substantial capital sums. With this influence goes a responsibility which analysts have accepted fully.

The education required coupled with the breadth and depth of their inquiries into companies, industries, and the national economy, qualify many analysts for leading positions in industry and finance. Thus analysts have in recent years become bank presidents and executive vice presidents; senior partners in broker-dealer firms and private banks; presidents of utility companies; financial vice presidents of industrial corporations; and corporate directors.

## THE OBJECTIVES AND METHODS OF THE ANALYST

Despite this heterogeneous background of occupation and activity, the common theme of all investment research is the determination of relative values of securities and their selection through appropriate portfolio policies. To make such determination, the analyst considers a wide variety of economic data (national and industry); industry data (technical and marketing); and company information (products, costs, earnings, capital structure, and management organization)—to name a few. The analyst must go to many sources to obtain such information, but he relies most heavily on the published reports of the company and direct contacts with management. After obtaining this vast array of information, the analyst must organize it into a logical pattern and evaluate the strengths and weakness of the company and the industry according to accepted principles of financial analysis. All of this is done in a comparative fashion—one company as against another—to reach a conclusion as to the best relative value available in the marketplace.

Investment research and the recommendation of particular securities are not ends in themselves. They contribute to the construction of investment portfolios to suit the diverse requirements of individuals and institutions. Thus portfolio policy is a proper extension of the analysts' field of endeavor. For portfolio management, the analyst investigates national economic trends, financial markets, monetary policy, and a host of political and social trends. These elements are sorted out and logically joined to formulate portfolio policy according to sound investment principles.

Any investment of capital aims to secure an income yield on that investment which is commensurate with the risk or safety of eventual return of the principal. Yield includes not only annual interest or dividends but also appreciation in capital value. The total return will tend to rise with uncertainty as to continuity of income and safety of principal.

In the final analysis, therefore, the investment analyst must project the future in order to estimate the probable income and safety of capital. Such projections may well run for long periods of time—35 to 40 years in the case of bonds. The analysis of historical experience is the best single guide to the probable trends of future events, but historical experience must be altered by judgment as to the impact of new developments. As a result, investment selection can never be completely scientific and precise in its approach as, say, accounting can; it is partly an art based on insight. Because of this fact and because people's insights vary widely, prices of securities—particularly of stocks—fluctuate widely. The analyst must be a market analyst as well as a security analyst to avoid some of the extremes of the marketplace.

Despite these problems, from which no investor of capital will ever be relieved, the financial analyst makes an important contribution to the economic process. That is to direct investment capital to the most productive areas of the economy. To the extent that the analyst is successful, waste of capital is avoided or minimized.

PROFESSIONAL ORGANIZATION OF ANALYSTS

The financial analyst has found it desirable to organize into a professional group just as others have done. The professional organization is known as The Financial Analysts Federation which is made up of 35 local societies of analysts in the United States and Canada. The oldest of these is The Investment Analysts Society of Chicago organized by 19 "statisticians" with various banks and brokerage firms back in 1925; more than one-half of these founders are still active in that society today. The largest society is New York which has almost 3,000 members; Boston, Chicago, and Philadelphia have memberships of 450 to 500. Some small societies have memberships of 50 or so. These societies are autonomous with regard to their local activities, but together they govern the national Federation through a board of directors and an executive committee.

Despite the wide range of size and character of financial communities represented, the standards of membership in the various societies are uniformly high. Typically, an analyst must have a minimum of three years' experience in investment research work and be currently engaged in that activity or in portfolio management or some closely related activity to become a member of one of the constituent societies. Some members may later change their occupation, but they are permitted to continue their membership. However, the vast majority of members are currently active in investment research and management. Persons engaged in selling securities are not considered eligible for membership. Because of the high order of analytical talent required to carry out their responsibilities, the members of the various societies as a group are well educated, serious, aggressive, and responsible.

The number of analysts has grown rapidly in the postwar period as a result of several factors: the increasing concentration of savings and investment in the hands of intermediaries such as pension funds, insurance trust departments, and mutual funds—all of which try to make investment decisions in a rational manner and, therefore, require organized research programs; the greatly increased acceptance of common stocks as a medium for conservative, long-term investment; and, finally, the greatly increased amount of capital available for investment. These factors have brought a substantial increase in demand for services of investment analysts and in their financial rewards. There are today over 8,250 members in constituent societies of The Financial Analysts Federation.

*The local society.* The principal unit of organization in The Financial Analysts Federation is the local society. Its primary activity is the presentation of programs of information and education for its members. The frequency of society meetings varies from every business day of the year in New York to once or twice a month in some of the smaller societies. Most meetings present corporation officials who discuss current developments and future prospects for their companies. The typical format of such a program is a formal presentation by the chief executive or chief financial officer of the company followed by an extensive question-and-answer period between the analysts and the official. Other members of the management team may be asked to join in the discussion. Managements of some of the large companies may find the numerous demands for appearances difficult to handle; but, on the whole, they believe presentations to analysts' societies a worthwhile expenditure of effort. Considering costs and competitive factors involved in making such presentations, most managements have adopted a policy of either employing all means necessary to make a good presentation or not accepting the invitation at all. Generally, program chairmen of the local society can be very helpful in guiding the company as to the best presentation.

With the number of societies and the number of meetings in a year, these programs provide an excellent means of communication between industry and the financial community. In addition to providing this flow of corporate financial information, the society programs include panels on current investment topics, economic forecasts, and related subjects. Just as valuable as the program itself is the opportunity for analysts to meet one another and exchange ideas. Perhaps more than in any other field of endeavor, investment analysts are willing and eager to exchange information and ideas.

*The national federation.* The Financial Analysts Federation is made up of the constituent societies and does not have individual members. It carries on activities of a professional nature at the national level. An annual convention is held in a different city each year with a local society as the host. These conventions have a full agenda that draws the complete attention of hard-working analysts. The program usually consists of conferences with managements of large companies, field trips to important industries in the area, the presentation of economic and financial forecasts, industry panels, and similar programs. The convention has grown to substantial size with the most recent convention in Chicago having an attendance of approximately 1,500.

The professional activities carried on by the Federation include the Financial Analysts Seminar, *The Financial Analysts Journal,* The Institute of Chartered Financial Analysts, Corporate Information Committee, Government Relations Committee, Professional Ethics and Education Committee, and a number of other standing committees.

The Financial Analysts Seminar is a one-week educational program held in conjunction with the University of Chicago School of Business. Its purpose is to provide senior analysts with a chance to get up to date on developments in economics and financial methodology. The Canadian Investment Seminar is a similar activity organized in 1963 to cater to the needs of Canadian analysts.

The publication issued by the Federation, *The Financial Analysts Journal,* is a bi-monthly professional journal containing articles with a wide range of interest to financial analysts and to others in the financial community. It has a circulation of about 12,000 copies per issue.

*The Institute of Chartered Financial Analysts.* This is the newest and most significant step in the professional growth of analysts. The Institute is a separately incorporated department of the federation. The objectives of the institute are as follows: "To foster higher educational standards in the field of financial analysis; to conduct examinations designed to test individual competence and skill in pertinent fields of knowledge; to recognize with the professional designation *Chartered Financial Analyst* (C.F.A.) persons who have met the standards established by the Institute for the professional ethical standards; and to stimulate research and the dissemination of educational materials."

A study of a program for the institute was begun in 1953 and was approved in 1959. The institute was established at the University of Virginia Graduate School of Business and has a member of that faculty as its director. In June of 1963 the first examinations were offered to senior analysts of a certain age, experience, and qualification; and 268 C.F.A. degrees were awarded in September of the same year to analysts throughout the United States and Canada. In 1964 the program will be in full operation with three examinations being offered. After the introductory period, all analysts will be required to pass the complete series of three examinations in order to obtain the C.F.A. It is anticipated that this designation will in time achieve a standing comparable to a C.P.A. designation for accountants.

The purpose of all such charters or certifications is to insure that each recipient possesses at least a minimum level of knowledge and is qualified to reason in a logical way about securities. He should be able to appraise adequately the analytical work of others. In itself the designation does not guarantee that any particular security recommendation will prove to be correct or that all charter analysts will become millionaires. As I have noted before, a final analysis of security selection has elements of art, since insight and judgment about future events are necessary to success. A law degree does not necessarily make a good lawyer, nor does an M.D. make a brilliant surgeon; however, they do insure mastery of a body of knowledge representing the most important elements of a profession. This should at least reduce the range of uncertainty and errors.

The Securities and Exchange Commission's Special Study of the Securities Markets has indicated a need for qualification for individuals active in various capacities in the securities industry, and it appears likely that analysts in research departments will need to pass some kind of qualification test administered by a self-regulatory agency such as the New York Stock Exchange. We hope that the C.F.A. designation will provide an adequate standard of qualification and that in time it will be universally adopted for investment research and management.

### THE WORK OF THE FEDERATION

The federation has three standing committees which are important to its professional functions. These are the Corporate Information Committee, the Government Relations Committee, and the Professional Ethics and Education Committee. In addition, there are other committees which have responsibilities concerned with the internal operations of the Federation.

The function of the Corporate Information Committee is "to work toward improvement in the quality and quantity of financial information disseminated by corporations; to make and publish surveys and studies with recommendations for improvement of corporate financial reporting." For many years the Corporate Information Committee has appointed special subcommittees to study reporting practices in selected industries and to make comparative reports thereon. Surveys of reporting practices in the banking, life insurance, copper, and other industries have been widely disseminated and have contributed to subsequent improvements in financial reporting. Obviously, a financial analyst can make better judgments if he has better information; so it is to his interest as well as the investing public generally to improve the quantity and quality of financial information. These industry studies continue to be an important part of the federation's work.

In 1962 the Corporate Information Committee published a 114-page monograph entitled *Corporate Reporting for The Professional Investor.* This report, written by Dr. Corliss D. Anderson of Northwestern University, a member of the committee, collected and summarized the reporting practices, methods of presentation, and type of information that analysts considered desirable to have in corporate annual reports. The report was sent to all members of the federation and to many company executives. The Corporate Information Committee now plans to evaluate corporate annual reports against criteria developed from this monograph. The best reports in particular industries will be awarded a certificate of excellence by the federation. We hope to have this program operative in early 1964.

The Government Relations Committee acts as liaison between the federation and Government agencies in Washington, particularly the Securities and Exchange Commission. As a professional organization, the federation does not take positions on proposed legislation except where its interests as a professional group are directly affected. Thus the federation is actively supporting the bill now before Congress which would increase the number of companies required to render financial reports to the Securities and Exchange Commission and regulate their proxy material among other things. The committee has also worked closely with the Securities and Exchange Commission on reporting requirements for corporations, this work dovetailing quite closely with the work of the Corporate Information Committee.

The Professional Ethics and Education Committee has the responsibility for establishing an appropriate code of conduct for analysts and for generally raising the ethical standards in the industry, albeit they are already very high. The federation has adopted a code of ethics, and practically all of the constituent societies have adopted it by reference. The individual societies are responsible for proper enforcement of the code, and they may be subject to penalty by the Federation if they fail to do so.

The basic concept of the code is a fourfold responsibility of analysts to the public; to customers, clients, and employers; to corporate management; and to associates and fellow analysts. The code reads as follows:

I. RESPONSIBILITY TO THE PUBLIC

The general public has the right to expect of the professional financial analyst technical competence and ability, honesty, and a high degree of integrity, objectivity in opinions expressed, and avoidance of exaggeration and misrepresentation. Moreover, the financial analyst should not resort to misleading and high pressure sales methods in solicitation of business, including extravagant claims and flamboyant advertising.

II. RESPONSIBILITY TO CUSTOMERS, CLIENTS, AND EMPLOYERS

Customers, clients, or employers of the analyst should expect and receive strict, undivided fidelity and loyalty to their particular interests, maintenance of complete confidence respecting their private affairs, and diligent and judicious effort in handling their business. Customers and clients are entitled to a clear understanding of the source of compensation received by the analyst or his organization in connection with services rendered to them. Customers, clients or employers are entitled to full disclosure respecting any conflict of interest on the part of the analyst, and the analyst should not enter into any business arrangement which might impair his ability to render unbiased and objective advice.

III. RESPONSIBILITY TO CORPORATE MANAGEMENT AND OTHER SOURCES OF INFORMATION

Corporations and others furnishing information to analysts have a right to expect of the professional analyst that any material so furnished will be reported accurately and not used in an inappropriate way or for any unfair personal advantage of the analyst. Information given to analysts by management on a confidential basis should be treated as such.

IV. RESPONSIBILITY TO ASSOCIATES AND FELLOW ANALYSTS

Associates and fellow analysts are entitled to expect of the analyst a high standard of professional conduct in all matters pertaining to competition with others in the field, relations with professional organizations, use of material, and terms and conditions of employment within his own organization. Every effort should be exerted to maintain unimpaired the professional status of the analyst in all aspects of his business relationships, and to uphold the honor and maintain the dignity of the profession.

Obviously, proper behavior does not result from adopting codes of ethics. It depends on the quality of people in the profession, their attitude toward life in general and their work in particular, and the general moral standards of its members. In these respects The Financial Analysts Federation is very fortunate, for the standards of behavior among analysts have been very high. Nevertheless, the code reminds each and every member of his responsibility to conduct his business in an appropriate manner and that he will be held accountable if he fails to do so.

# WHAT THE ANALYST WANTS IN CORPORATE REPORTS •

CORLISS D. ANDERSON

CORPORATIONS HAVE COME A LONG, long way in the past 35 years or so in making information available for the use of stockholders and the investment fraternity generally. The widespread ownership of corporations makes better and more timely corporate disclosure of pertinent data more necessary than ever.

Of growing importance to the professional investor is the heavy trusteeship responsibility which many of them now carry in the management of huge investments, running into the billions of dollars—sums that are no less than the balance sheet footings of many of our largest corporations. Which is to say, investment management responsibilities have grown to the size of corporate management burdens, though different in their nature. Increasingly, the courts have tended to hold investment managers—and particularly trustees—to a higher standard of knowledge and stewardship.

Corporate management should be aware of the importance to the professional investor of being able to make comparisons of similar enterprises and should make every effort to make financial figures comparable or provide the supplemental information which will allow financial analysts to make them comparable.

What specific kinds of information are professional investors interested in? What does the financial analyst want to know? We shall discuss a number of areas and attempt to summarize the type of information included in each.

---

CORLISS D. ANDERSON is Chairman, Finance Department, School of Business, Northwestern University, Evanston, Illinois, and Chairman of the Corporate Information Committee of the Financial Analysts Federation.

It should be borne in mind, however, that not all of the following suggestions apply to any one company. But it is hoped that even those companies in the forefront of good corporate reporting practice will find some of these comments of value.

This, then, is a summary of the areas in which financial analysts are interested. Each company must decide for itself what parts of this information are appropriate for it to communicate, what items should not be revealed because they are of a nature to give comfort or aid to competitors, and what the best methods of communicating the information are. In this way, it will take a long step toward putting its relations with professional investors on a sound basis.

Parenthetically, let it be noted here that some companies such as public utilities and railroads now prepare supplements to the annual report which carry information for the particular use of financial analysts. This practice saves the company the trouble of sending detailed information to many who would not be interested in it and yet makes it available to those professional investors who are primarily interested in it and ask for it. A statement to the effect that such information can be obtained from the company and a post card for requesting it should be part of the annual report in such cases.

## GENERAL ECONOMIC FACTORS

*The company's business.* A quick way to inform shareholders of the business of a company is to give a sales breakdown by products (in natural groupings) and also by the types of customers or industries served. This kind of information serves to interpret a company to its owners. Companies should beware of giving a false impression as to the importance of a specific product or project. Sometimes one would get the impression that a certain project (or product) is of major importance by a casual perusal but on detailed analysis discover that it is relatively insignificant.

Further, analysts would like information on the correlation or relationship of the company's business with specific economic facts and trends, where the correlation exists. For example, a company's sales may correlate closely with freight car loadings, and this could be revealed. Some companies are able to relate their sales and profits to certain peculiar and tangible fundamental conditions and influences; this knowledge would be of interest to a professional investor and, if known, would often save time and effort in management explanations. The earnings surprises would be fewer; judging future earnings could be accomplished perhaps within narrower limits, and investors would have a better understanding of the particular economic framework or pattern within which the company operates—and thus a better conception of management's problems.

*Product price trends.* When it is feasible, analysts would like to know the year's trend in product prices, or the average level as compared with the level of the previous year or years. This enables analysts to allocate the dollar sales gains between increased unit volume and unit prices. If the company's business involves several lines, then separate price indexes could well be given for major groups of products. A discussion of the factors determining future price trends in the ensuing year or years is always, of course, welcome and useful. Also, some comments might be made on the outlook for "costs," especially if the company is a big user of industrial materials which fluctuate in price from time to time.

*Tariffs.* Within the last decade many American corporations have found themselves in a broad stream of international trade, either directly by an extension of their own operations or because competitive products manufactured in other countries have flowed into the United States.

It would be helpful to investors if companies would give information on the amounts of tariffs involved as well as the changes (downward, mostly, it is assumed) in amount or degree of these tariffs. This can be a complicated subject, but only a relatively simple statement would serve the purpose intended.

*Foreign operations.* Inasmuch as many companies are now or will in the future be importantly involved in foreign operations, it would be of interest to investors to know the capital investment in these operations and the sales and net earnings, as well as the income taxes deducted in arriving at the net earnings. In particular, the amount of foreign earnings which are not consolidated should be made clear. Other matters of significant interest are losses due to changes in the rate of exchange; the degree to which earnings may be withdrawn and any other legal restrictions on the free flow of funds; the effect of United States legislation on tax rates on foreign earnings, either retained in foreign countries or paid to the United States parent company as dividends. Foreign investment and operations have always been subject to varying interpretations by professional analysts. If facts are laid out plainly, investors can place their own interpretations and evaluations on them.

## OPERATING AND FINANCIAL MATTERS

*Fundamental company policies.* Many companies have a business creed or a code of ethics for their executives and their employees, not only in their relations one with the other but with respect to their customers, their communities, their suppliers. They may also have fundamental policies as to the type of expansion—vertical or horizontal—or as to foreign operations. If such policies exist, describing them in general terms at least would be valuable.

*Research and development.* Most analysts would like companies to report separately the amounts of money spent in each year for research and development. It is true that the definition of the term "research and development" is not always the same among various companies. However, the National Science Foundation's definition is appropriate: "Technological research and development is an activity in basic and applied research in the sciences and in engineering, and it is the design and development of prototypes and processes. Excluded from this definition are routine product testing, market research, sales promotion, sales service, research in social sciences or psychology, and other nontechnological activities or technical services." Research and development expense might well be broken down into (1) the amount spent on company-sponsored activities and (2) the amount expended (and therefore reimbursed) on Government- or customer-financed research.

Other data which can be of value to analysts in this aspect of a company's affairs are the number of research people with advanced degrees, the number of technical papers prepared by company people for scientific journals, and the number of patents issued to the company during the year.

Nevertheless, the *results* of research are the important consideration, not the size of the expense. Not all fields of industry carry a high potential for research activities; on the other hand, many do. Some companies in the more productive types of business tell shareholders what proportion of their present products (or sales) were unknown five or ten years ago. They say, for example, that 45 per cent of current sales are in items not produced ten years ago.

*Marketing and advertising.* In many cases, analysts want more information on the marketing setup or on how important the marketing setup is to specific companies. Companies that are heavily dependent upon marketing operations should find it worthwhile to discuss rather fully this aspect of their business.

One of the variable items of expense from year to year is the amount spent for advertising. If advertising "pays"—and most people do believe that well-executed advertising does pay off—then a drastic cut in advertising expense in any one or two years may not only not "save money" but actually cost the company sales and profits then or later. Which is to say, investors should look to the advertising expense for an indication of nonrecurring savings if a company has attempted to minimize a drop in earnings by cutting its advertising drastically.

Although relatively few managements inform analysts of their companies' advertising budgets, other agencies are gathering and publicizing these figures each year. Publishers Information Bureau is one of the main compilers of such material. Most any advertising man can find out how big a company's advertising budget was this year, or last year—and even what it will be next year, subject to change, of course.

*Nature and cost of acquisitions.* The cost of acquisitions should be made public. The merger of two *large* companies is always accompanied by wide publicity as to the terms of the merger—namely, the cost of the acquisition in number and ratio of shares of stock. More often than not, the merging companies prepare a prospectus which not only defines the terms but gives detailed information on the acquired company's business, properties, balance sheet, as well as earnings statements for several years. Acquisitions for *cash,* for some unexplained reason, are often consummated without the cost figure being made public. Acquisitions of importance are material in consequence and not only should be defined as to cost but should be explained in terms of past sales and earnings and balance sheet and how the acquired business fits into the acquiring company's future plans. Some sellers object to this information (especially the purchase price) being made public. This objection seems minor compared with the advantages of disclosure to perhaps thousands of shareholders.

*Quantity and quality of natural resources.* Those companies having timberlands or natural resources such as oil, potash, and coal often purchase a portion of their requirements from neighboring owners. It would be helpful for an analyst to know each year the quantity purchased from others and the quantity taken from the company's own resources. Another figure is the estimated growth in a resource during the year, either through natural growth—such as timber—or through discovery of new and more efficient extractive processes or better methods of estimating the amounts and quality of the resource involved. The final figure which is essential is the estimate of the remaining resources owned by the company at the year's close. The data are generally estimates only and must be so considered.

*Plans for capital expenditures.* Many analysts would find information on capital expenditures—to the extent that the board of directors has authorized them—to be of value. The proposed expenditures may, of course, extend beyond the year and might well be classified as to specific projects if the company is operating in several types of business. Another item of interest to investors is some indication of the cost savings and greater efficiency expected of these new facilities. If the facilities are for added capacity, a company might want to discuss the percentage by which enlarged sales may result—assuming the capacity can be utilized. If the capital expenditures are in lines of new endeavor or in fields materially different from the company's established business, this story should be told clearly. It probably goes without saying that a story on proposed or estimated capital expenditures should be checked for its value as competitive information. Reference might also be made to the approximate amount of internally generated funds which would likely be accounted for by depreciation and other noncash charges.

*Future financing.* Analysts are interested in knowing the types and likely amounts of financing in the next year or two. Some companies, especially public utilities, are able to spell this out for several years ahead. Obviously, the investment markets of the future make any plans subject to change. If a company believes that there is little likelihood of the need for new financing (especially common stock) within the next few years, this might be indicated—all subject to change, of course. This matter of financing may well lead a company management to review for the shareholders its philosophy on the kind of corporate financial condition management wishes to maintain or achieve for the company. This could involve many factors, including degree of funded debt, short-term debt, long leases, use of preferred stock, and others.

*Source and application of funds.* A source-and-application-of-funds statement is another item of interest to analysts. There are many variations today in such statements; uniformity among companies is not a requisite for analytical purposes.

*Method of consolidation of accounts.* A company should also make clear the method of consolidation of its balance sheet and income account. It should indicate by name the subsidiaries which are not consolidated (and sometimes, perhaps, those which *are* consolidated) in order that there be no question of what is excluded or included in the consolidation. Does "consolidated" mean to include all majority-owned companies; only domestic majority-owned; domestic and Canada; or domestic, Canada, Western Hemisphere, and so on? What is meant by the use of terms such as subsidiary, affiliate, associate? At the expense of perhaps redundancy, these matters should be made clear on the balance sheet itself or on explanatory notes to the balance sheet.

*Dividend policy.* Inasmuch as the most tangible reward to shareholders is the dividend paid periodically, reference should be made to the dividend policy, if one has been established by the board of directors. This means the size of the cash dividend in relation to earnings and to the need to retain earnings, the matter of stock dividends of small size in lieu of cash disbursements, and large stock dividends or stock splits. If there is no policy, it presumably could not be described; if there is, then it could be defined for what it is, subject of course to change as circumstances require.

## BALANCE SHEET ITEMS

*Marketable securities (current assets).* It is assumed, unless otherwise indicated, that "marketable securities" are debt obligations and that the maturities are not more than one year in length. If they are not debt obligations, they should certainly be defined clearly. The domestic securities should be broken down into two general classifications:

1. Taxable—United States Government and corporates.
2. Nontaxable—municipal and state bonds, if material in amount.

Foreign government issues should be so indicated. The basis of carrying value should be clear; "book" and "market" should both be shown if there is a substantial difference.

*Investments (other than current assets).* If significant in amount, these other investments should be described as to amounts and in some detail:

1. Bonds, notes, and other advances (issuer, rate, and maturity).
2. Preferred stocks (issuer, rate, and so on).
3. Common stocks by name.

There is good reason in some cases, especially in the case of marketable securities, to make a table of investments, showing book and market. We should segregate domestic and foreign. In the event affiliates or nonconsolidated subsidiaries are involved, the material amounts should be segregated in some detail, as above, including the company's equity in affiliates as indicated on the affiliates' books.

*Trade receivables.* Gross amount, provision for possible losses, and net amount of receivables should be given: segregation into United States Government, customers, and affiliates is desirable. If longer-term receivables (such as installment contracts) are included as current assets, the portion not expected to be collected in one year should be clearly noted.

*Inventories.* Inventories should be divided among several natural categories, depending on the type of company. Generally it is possible to use:

1. Raw materials.
2. In process.
3. Finished goods.
4. Supplies (operating and maintenance).

The method of valuation needs to be made clear, that is, LIFO, FIFO, market, cost, average cost, and so forth. Where companies are carrying a portion of inventories on LIFO and the balance on FIFO, an understandable explanation should accompany the figures.

*Fixed assets.* It is assumed that fixed assets are carried at cost unless otherwise indicated. A company may, in good conscience, indicate that certain fixed assets have a current (estimated) market value of approximately twice (or X times) their carrying value. This refers to timberlands, oil reserves or other deposits, or real estate. The matter would need to be significant and explained carefully. "Insurance values" would likewise be interesting if they could properly be keyed into book values. We should think in terms of round-amount figures rather than "to the penny" amounts in connection with these insurance appraisals. Categories of fixed assets should be separated into principal items, with reserves (depreciation, depletion, and amortization) applied to each category. In the event a company leases some of its fixed assets to others, some indication of the amount of such leased assets should be indicated. Companies operating in countries other than the United States may clarify their position by indicating the amounts of the several types of gross and net assets in each country, or perhaps by hemisphere.

*Depreciation, depletion, amortization reserves.* For the guidance of professional investors, a company should define its policy of writing off its fixed assets as well as intangible assets. This information is given in some detail in the 10-K reports and could well be summarized. The three items—depreciation, depletion, and amortization—should be discussed and shown separately in the balance sheet and in the income account. Any change in policy deserves to be made clear to shareholders; the effects of such policy changes should be approximated as to dollar amounts. The 1962 revision of "Bulletin F" makes the information requested here especially important at this time. "Investment credit" legislation calls for additional information, to the end that shareholders are able to understand how the matter is being handled in the balance sheet and income account.

*Intangible assets.* Basis of cost should be indicated, and it should be broken down (if substantial) into: patents, copyrights, goodwill, trademarks and brand names, research and development (if capitalized), and other categories. The basis of amortizing these intangible assets should be shown.

*Funded debt.* In the decade following World War II, corporations enjoyed comparatively low borrowing costs on long-term money. Since 1956 we have had sporadic periods of high rates and stringent indenture provisions. Analysts like to know the details. For example, a company might discuss funded debt, describing each issue in substantially these terms: amount, interest rate, and maturity. It should indicate the form of security: mortgage bonds, debenture, subordinated debenture, and collateral trust (collateral should be defined). Call provisions (sinking funds, as a whole or in part, or otherwise) should be treated. Any special provisions should be mentioned, such as GMAC 5s, 1977, which are callable at par in case of war when automobile production is halted by Government decree. Sinking fund provisions (with a table showing amount of maturities in each of the next five years) and also the degree to which sinking fund requirements have been anticipated should be indicated. If held privately—for example, by insurance companies—this should also be so indicated. Professional investors would like to know restrictions as to additional long-term debt, maintenance of working capital, cash dividend payments, long-term leases, and mergers. To the extent there are any restrictions, the company should indicate approximately its estimate of the amounts by which the actual figures exceed the requirements. Convertibility, with conversion features, spelled out clearly covering the next ten years if the rate of conversion changes is another item of interest. If income bonds are outstanding, their provisions as to payment of interest should be stated clearly.

*Long-term leases.* Long-term leases have replaced bond indebtedness in many companies; investors should be in a position to appraise the financial impact of leases. While modern accounting and finance thus far have not devised an acceptable way to show a definite dollar figure in the balance sheet as a liability, there should be an adequate summary of the leases along the lines as recommended to the Securities and Exchange Commission by the Government Relations Committee of the Financial Analysts Federation. It might be divided as follows:

1. Aggregate total lease rental payments actually made in the years reported.
2. Aggregate amounts contracted for and payable (excluding conditional rentals) in the year following the reporting period and in the four successive five-year periods beyond.
3. The aggregate amounts contracted for and payable after 21 years and the period over which such payments are due.
4. A statement as to the nature of the assets leased, including classification as between realty and other assets.

In the event the company has a subsidiary real estate corporation (not consolidated), the data above outlined should be divided in a manner that will indicate the rentals to outside unrelated owners and the rentals "within the family." Parenthetically, the indebtedness, if any, of the unconsolidated subsidiary should also be shown clearly at some point, together with a suitable description of the debt (and how, if at all, it is guaranteed by the parent) as well as the properties or assets which are being leased to the parent company. In suggesting this aspect of the ownership (and the leasing) of unconsolidated subsidiaries, we recognize that there is a duplication of "parent company rentals" and "subsidiary company income and indebtedness." Where of sufficient size, the sale and leaseback of a property should be described, including amount of proceeds, profit or loss on the sale, terms of the lease such as options for extending the lease and the rentals for the several periods involved.

*Pension funds.* One of the imponderables in security analysis is the contingent liability known as the unfunded cost of past service. It is obvious that if company *A* and company *B* are of the same size; with the same number of employees, wage levels, length of past service, the same pension benefits, and so on; and company *A* has completely provided for cost of past service—and company *B* has an unfunded past service cost estimated at, say, $35 million—then company *A* is better off than company *B*.

We recognize that the unfunded cost of past service is only an actuarial estimate and, further, that there are many variables, making an exact evaluation of the "contingent liability" almost impossible, such as (1) the assumed rate of interest versus the actual earned; (2) the type of investment made with the contributions (common stocks purchased at low prices, bonds at high prices, or vice versa); (3) when the fund was started; and (4) the longevity of the employees. This does not mean, however, that companies should not be very explicit in their reporting each year of the amount expensed, so that investors can measure the influence of pension costs upon earnings, year by year.

*Preferred or senior stock.* As is true of funded debt, a preferred stock ranks ahead of the common; thus the common shareholder (as well as the preferred shareholder) may well be interested in viewing each year the provisions of the preferred stock. Preferred or senior stock should be described as to:

1. Amounts and dividend rates of the several series outstanding.
2. Call prices, now and later, voluntary and involuntary.
3. Sinking fund requirements, if any, and how far ahead they are met.
4. If they are privately held.
5. The number of shareholders.
6. Restrictions (in bond or loan agreements) on the payment of preferred dividends, with statement as to leeway or "cushion" now existing.
7. Charter provisions of preferred stock which limit the sale of additional preferred or the issuance of additional funded debt or the making of long-term leases.
8. Percentage of outstanding shares required to change the charter provisions.
9. Dividend arrearages, if any.
10. Voting power of the preferred.
11. Any special or unusual provisions.

12. Convertible features, if any, stated clearly and covering the next ten years.

*Common stock.* The company should discuss legal restrictions on dividends and, in such cases, should indicate the amount of "free" surplus that legally would be available at the fiscal year-end for dividend payments, either preferred or common. Working capital restrictions on dividends may be involved also.

## INCOME STATEMENT

*Sales, orders, backlog of orders.* Companies should be specific as to what constitutes sales, especially in those industries which, like the automobile manufacturers, have large dealer organizations. Building contractors or manufacturers of large equipment requiring more than one accounting year to complete their work present special problems in defining sales. Some companies report quarterly on orders received, shipments, and remaining backlog of orders. This is especially appropriate in those industries which require lead time in filling orders, such as those involved in heavy electrical apparatus and construction equipment. This disclosure of information should be prepared realistically and on a comparable basis from year to year.

*Government contracts.* When Government work is relatively sizable, a company should devote some attention to the nature of the work (assuming it may be revealed), the year's sales, what basis (cost-plus or competitive bidding), the accounting used in defining sales and earnings, and the depreciation and amortization adopted in arriving at earnings. One major consideration is whether the company uses the "completed contract" basis in figuring sales—and particularly earnings—or whether the company calculates its sales and earnings on a "per cent of completion" basis. (This comment applies to nonGovernment contracts as well, of course, if they transcend fiscal years.) The company should indicate whether it is greatly dependent on one or two Government programs or whether its Government sales are widely diffused over the whole procurement effort. This gives shareholders some evidence of the potential vulnerability of the work being of a nonrecurring nature. The status of renegotiation should also be clearly stated—to the extent that it is possible.

*Abnormal variations in Federal income tax rates.* It is well recognized that reports to shareholders often carry income accounts wherein the Federal income tax rate is considerably less than 52 per cent—the effective rate at the time of writing. This is particularly true in the case of natural-resource companies such as oil, gas, sulphur, potash, lumber, and coal, because of the depletion allowances applicable in these cases. However, when a company (not in the above category) shows a tax that is not approximately 52 per cent (the present rate) of the income before taxes, an appropriate explanation should be given; or the income information should be complete enough for an investor to figure out the reasons himself. The impact on tax rates, if any, which are the result of the "investment credit" enacted into law deserves a clear explanation.

*Sources of earnings.* More unusual but of course more significant than a breakdown of sales is a breakdown of earnings. Most managements will answer the question, "Is each division of the company operating in the black?" But very few will indicate the profitability of each division or of each wholly owned subsidiary. This information is presumably guarded zealously in order not to attract competitors to the highly profitable lines, among other reasons. It is not easy to refute this argument, although many management weaknesses and errors—especially in acquisitions—are perhaps hidden quietly in the consolidated income account. There are also inherent difficulties in allocating costs among divisions. However, approximations are made by companies internally. The real question relates to the return on investment in each division or subsidiary—and there is much to be said for disclosing divisional net earnings in this manner. This can be done by indicating, first, the overall return on the company's total investment and, then, naming the divisions that earned less than the "average" return and those which earned a rate higher than the company average.

*Nonrecurring earnings and expenses.* Management and the accounting profession can be helpful in separating out of the income account those items of income and expense which are believed to be nonrecurring or are of a nonoperating nature. We have in mind material charges or credits (including income taxes) relating to a previous year's operations; profits or losses on the sale of assets; uninsured losses due to floods, fire, earthquakes. An income tax credit of significant amount—for any reason—should be explained carefully so that the investor can make an adjustment in the reported earnings.

In addition to items which are reasonably definite in amount, there are some which require estimating—such as start-up expense, unusually heavy research and development costs, strike costs, moving expense, introduction of new products, and others. Shareholders ought to be advised of these—at least in round figures—if they are material in amount and if they are expected not to be of a recurring nature. Windfalls on the income side should be described, too, with a view to segregating them from "true" recurring earnings from operations. The practice of companies of alluding to a previous year's results when comparing them with the current year and bringing to light *for the first time* the unusual or nonrecurring profit "earned" in the earlier year is to be deplored. Earnings summaries or releases to the financial press should exclude material nonrecurring profits or losses in computing net earnings per share. Material nonrecurring items should be reported separately.

*An informative income account.* It is impossible to suggest *one* income account which will serve all investment analysis purposes because there is more than one way to view the expenses of an enterprise—and enterprises differ in their character. Fully aware, then, of the difficulties, I suggest the income account items which are generally important to the financial analyst in reviewing the operations of a company—*assuming* that the items are substantial in amount:

A. SALES AND INCOME

1. Sales—broken down into sales of:
   Product.
   Parts.
   Supplies.
   Services.
   Rentals.
   Miscellaneous.
2. Other or nonoperating income:
   Royalties.
   Interest.
   Dividends.
   Miscellaneous.
3. Nonrecurring income (or expense), such as:
   Profit or loss on sales of assets.
   Tax refunds, assessments, or tax-loss carry-forwards.
   Storm losses.
   Litigation.
   Renegotiation.
   Foreign exchange fluctuation.
   Proceeds of life insurance.
   Moving expense.
   Start-up expense.
   Savings in income taxes due to deductible gift.

B. ITEMS OF OUTGO

1. Employment costs:
   Wages and salaries.
   Bonus compensation.
   Payroll taxes.
   Pension retirement plans.

1. Costs of production:
   Labor and supplemental costs.
   Materials.
   Maintenance and repairs.

Insurance and fringe benefits.
Other.
2. Materials and services.
3. Rent.
4. Taxes (excluding income taxes) with excise taxes shown separately if included in "Sales."

Rent.
Taxes (excluding income taxes).
Other.
2. Selling expense:
Advertising.
Other.
3. Administration.
4. Research and development.

5. Noncash charges:
Depreciation.
Depletion.
Amortization.
6. Interest and debt discount amortization.
7. Other charges.
8. Income taxes.
State.
Federal.
Foreign.
9. Net earnings.

This outline can only be suggestive and is intended to be just that. Only when the items are material in amount should they be disclosed as separate entries. Obviously, the type of business will dictate the choice of points 1 to 4 in the above "Items of Outgo."

*Ten-year summary.* Most corporations are now offering at least a ten-year summary of financial and other data. These summaries are most helpful and should include the following:

1. Complete income account data, broken down into items carried in the most recent annual report.
2. Breakdown of sales by type of customers or industries served, or by products.
3. When a corporation has been acquiring other substantial companies, a ten-year pro forma income account.
4. Selected balance sheet items.
5. Source and application of funds statement.
6. Adjusted per share earnings and dividends, showing the basis of adjustment as well as explanation of distortions caused by the issuance of shares for cash or property. Also, the earnings per share figures should exclude substantial nonrecurring profits or losses.

7. Per cent earned on the company's net worth.
8. Operating statistics: these are not normally supplied in the investment services.
9. Notes on the income-account summary indicating years of unusual occurrences, such as strikes, catastrophes, nonrecurring charges, or windfalls. It is very important in such summaries that interpretive information be included; otherwise, the "stone cold" figures may actually be misleading to one attempting to analyze the data.
10. Economic or business data, as they may relate to a company's activities.

EMPLOYEE, MANAGEMENT, AND SHAREHOLDER DATA

*Employees.* Many corporations give but little attention in reports to employee matters. However, there are a number of significant points which can be covered. They are of basic importance to investors but should be described in meaningful rather than legalistic language. Suggested topics are as follows:

1. Description of company policies with respect to employee relations.
2. Number of employees; data on number of employees by various periods of service; employee turnover data, where meaningful.
3. Unionization, names of unions, duration of union contracts, expiration dates, and so on. Description of wage settlements with as definite as possible absolute or percentage figures on wage increases; effects and durations of any strikes during the year.
4. Training programs, college recruitment programs, scholarship activities.
5. Wage and salary data, profit-sharing, bonus plans, pension and fringe benefits.
6. Stock ownership by employees, purchase plan, per cent of employees participating, and their total holdings of shares.
7. Employment contracts of officers or directors.
8. Any other matters of significance.

*Management.* The cornerstone of every company is management, and somehow our body of corporate information seems to be the least helpful on this score.

The board of directors' business or professional affiliations should be revealed each year. Shareholders are electing these men to represent them in choosing management and in setting policy; it is a natural and legitimate question to ask who they are. In regard to officers and top management, some companies have from time to time published separate pamphlets on their management team for circulation among shareholders. By and large, these descriptions are helpful and especially so if they incorporate data on age, education, experience, scientific attainments, and other facts of material consequence. Another facet of this subject is how the management team's responsibilities are divided; an organization chart can be illuminating. Probably the most important ingredients in management are difficult to portray—namely, the spirit, drive, native ability, and personal qualities that make for a company's success. And, lastly, what is being done to perpetuate the strong management team—into another generation? Stock options ought also to be shown clearly.

*Type of shareholder ownership.* Proxy statements carry complete information on the number of shares owned by each of the directors of a (listed) company as of a given date each year. Analysts are divided in their appraisal of the importance of director ownership. It is believed, however, that a sizable majority of professional investors prefer that directors (and management personnel) have a substantial ownership of company shares rather than a nominal amount. Further, when it is observed that the directors are selling or buying stock on balance, analysts are inclined to weigh this as an investment consideration.

Now, as to the type of ownership of the company as a whole, we are less sure of the meaning of complete information. The fact that more women's names are on shareholder lists than men's names is perhaps most meaningful to the persons who prepare annual reports. Also, we would guess that the large holdings in nominees' names might well include more men than women. If a high percentage of stock is held in brokers' names, the question arises as to how "well placed" the shares may be. If institutions, foundations, insurance companies, and investment trusts are large holders, it would be presumed that the shares have an investment rather than a speculative status.

# THE FINANCIAL ANALYST CALLS ON MANAGEMENT •

FRANK B. SMITH

THE VISITING ANALYST HAS BECOME a post-World War II phenomenon. With the emergence of "research" as the magic word in selling securities, investment advice, mutual funds, and so on, virtually every organization of any size in business now has a research department. And by far the most popular form of research is the field trip. The effectiveness of a field trip varies widely with the organization and with the individual. Many analysts believe that the principal purpose is to evaluate the management. Most experienced analysts, however, look on the field trip only as a tool for obtaining information about the company. (There are, after all, very few individuals who have the prescience to determine whether a man is a good manager in the space of a brief, or even an extended, interview.)

It is information that the analyst is seeking. What kind of information? The chapter in the Value Line Investment Survey Training Manual on field trips contains over 15 closely typed, single-spaced pages of sample questions for use in interviewing company officials. Obviously, many of these do not apply to all companies. Just as obviously, many possible situations are not covered by the samples.

Basically, our analysts are instructed to seek information that will enable them to make reasoned forecasts under a given set of economic conditions of the profits (and dividends) of the particular industry and of the company relative to that industry. Such information naturally covers a

---

FRANK B. SMITH is Associate Research Director, The Value Line Investment Survey, New York, New York.

host of factors. The careful analyst will have thoroughly studied all recently published information about the company and will generally be seeking unpublished information: the whys, the intangibles, the future developments. This is not to say that the analyst should necessarily be given "inside" information, or that he be given information which would be damaging from a competitive standpoint (though the latter type is becoming less and less meaningful as lines between industries become more and more blurred and product lines become more mixed).

We shall discuss a few of the areas of information in which the analyst is interested. These are assumed to be for an analyst who is learning about the industry and the company for the first time. The general area of background information, for example, need hardly be covered by the experienced industry specialist. Similarly, the extent of detailed answers will be affected by the size and complexity of the company.

*Industry background.* The analyst needs information on the major economic, political, and technological forces influencing the industry and the company. Some examples of economic subjects that might be investigated are the degree of price elasticity; the importance of brands; the impact of advertising; the amount of capital investment required; principal sources of supply of raw materials; distribution costs, fixed costs, and development costs; the major influences on product prices and their long-term trends. As far as political factors are concerned, the analyst would probably want to know the trend of antitrust activity, if any; special tax considerations; policies of any regulatory body concerned and their impact; dependence on government business; and trends in procurement. As to technological forces, the analyst needs to know basically the pace of technological obsolescence; the degree of profitability of new products and how long they last; and the extent to which research costs must rise just to stay even competitively. Obviously, the foregoing examples only scratch the surface of a full background study, but they are at least illustrative of the areas of interest. We expect our analysts to be real "students" of the industry.

*Company background.* In this general category, the analysts are interested in obtaining historical information that might be useful in assessing the future. Also included in this area are the general economic aspects of the company and the company's philosophy and policies.

From the historical standpoint, for example, the analysts would want an explanation of how the company evolved into its present nature, the impact of previous antitrust settlements, how changes in tariffs affected sales and earnings, the significance of the introduction of synthetic raw materials, the impact of mergers, and so forth.

As far as policies are concerned, perhaps a list of some of the areas of interest would be useful. Among them are the following:

1. Dividends: pay-out proportions, extras, stock dividends and splits.
2. Pricing: breadth of lines, new products, reaction to cuts.
3. Acquisitions: integration, diversification, cash or stock.
4. Permanent financing: debt, stock, convertible securities.
5. Temporary financing: inventories and receivables.
6. Management development: retirement age and promotion from within.
7. Research: basic research, product and process development.
8. Sales: organization and credit.
9. Accounting: accelerated depreciation and intangibles.
10. Stock options.
11. Retirement plans.
12. Government business.
13. Capital outlays.
14. Return desired on new investment.

It can be seen that what is really desired here is an insight into how the company might react under a given set of circumstances.

From an economic standpoint, much of the information will, of course, be derived from the background discussion of the industry. However, such details as trends in the company's product mix, specific factors affecting the company's own supply and demand situation, plant capacity data, and share of the market trends are examples of subjects of interest in this category.

*Current information.* Presumably, much of the material discussed in the foregoing will be covered only in the initial interview with the analyst, though from time to time some review or discussion of one or more points may be desirable. Each time an analyst calls on a company, however, there are many points of current interest which he will wish to check. Here, too, our analysts are instructed to go behind the figures where possible. If profit margins are wider, for example, is it because of higher prices, greater volume, improved efficiency (from what?), or some other factor?

We are interested in current trends of prices, costs, volume, and so on. What causes them? Will they continue? Is a reversal in the offing? As can be realized, the analyst's most difficult, and at the same time most valuable, function is the accurate forecast of the timing and impact of the reversal of any trend. It is relatively easy to project the status quo or continuation of an existing trend. But picking the turning points, in advance, is most rewarding to investors. I have listed below some of the information the analyst needs about current and prospective developments:

1. Backlog (if applicable): amount and trend of orders relative to (*a*) shipments and (*b*) year-earlier period.
2. Prices: recent and future direction, relationship between list and realized, changes in capacity-demand relationship.
3. Sales: impact of competitor's new product or new promotion; impact of own programs and new products; changes in the mix, experienced or expected—by product classification, market, and price category ("high end versus low end"); share of market changes.
4. Labor costs: contract expiration dates, industry trends, likelihood of strikes, prices to offset increases.
5. Raw materials price trends.
6. Other significant cost changes.
7. Inventory situation: hedging against supplier strike, inventory losses or profits, inventory in hands of dealers, and so on.
8. Nonrecurring costs, experienced or expected.
9. Changes in working capital: cash position, receivables and payables, near-term debt maturities.
10. New financing and other changes in capital structure.
11. Capital outlays contemplated.

In addition to these areas, of course, there are many questions peculiar to each company or industry: the impact of a cold wave on a gas company's earnings; the status of a company's new drug before the Food and Drug Administration, and so on. These questions will arise from the analyst's study of the company. It goes without saying, of course, that if any important area is overlooked by the analyst, he will appreciate it being brought to light. We ask our analysts to ask near the conclusion of the interview for the executive's views on "the company's major problems over the next year or so" and "the company's most significant opportunities."

*Competitors.* Throughout the sample questions used by our analysts are questions about competitors. This is not done with a view toward eliciting unfavorable information, but frequently answers about competitors are from a different standpoint. Is there price leadership? By whom? Is it effective? What are the relative competitive positions in a general way? Which companies are increasing their shares of the market? Which are decreasing? Why? What are the greatest strengths and weaknesses of principal competitors? Who are the innovators? Who, if any, are the copiers? Who are the quality producers? Who are the mass marketers? Objective answers to these questions, properly synthesized, can be invaluable in the analyst's next visit to the competitors.

The plant tour can be a useful adjunct to interviews with company officials. It tends to put in perspective what the company "does for a living." In general, however, we believe such tours should be relatively brief and need not ordinarily be repeated. The analyst can never become expert and would, in our opinion, have a great deal of difficulty evaluating, say, the comparative efficiency of two similar plants. There are exceptions, of course, but most analysts are not engineers and have no production experience. For the most part, therefore, the plant tour is only educational; and since the average analyst is not equipped to grasp more than the rudiments of the operation, the tour's part in the total educational process is better kept to a minimum. Of course, an analyst of the steel business should know what a steel mill looks like, and insofar as possible, he should understand how it operates.

These, then, are the highlights of the type of information the analyst seeks on visits to companies. If he is competent and conscientious, he will have done his homework and will not needlessly go over information publicly available, although he may inquire as to why certain things occurred or ask for more detail. He does not generally seek "inside" information but would undoubtedly consider it in his evaluation, if it is given to him. He will, even so, generally treat the executive's remarks in confidence if requested to do so. He is interested in company forecasts, if available, and the reasoning behind them but will in general make his own forecast in any case. He will try not to waste time in minor, duplicative, or simply foolish questions. He wishes to learn the facts about the company as well as any outsider can do so, and anything that can be done to assist him serves the company's interest as well as the analyst's.

# GROUND RULES FOR TALKING WITH ANALYSTS •

**O. GLENN SAXON, Jr.**

THE MAN RESPONSIBLE FOR RELATIONS with professional investors and financial analysts may sometimes feel overwhelmed by the amount of advice given him about these contacts. As the person responsible for this work in General Electric Company, I have attempted to set forth for myself a number of clear-cut ground rules. They are the result of experience and are offered here in the hope that others may find them of use in their professional investor relations.

In the first place, in its relations with the professional investment community, a company has two key objectives:

1. To provide better, more accurate information to financial analysts, so they will base their appraisals of a company and a company's shares more on factual and real information about the company and less on rumor, speculation, and hunch.
2. To encourage the investment community to transmit this better and more accurate information far more aggressively to the many millions of Americans who have the financial ability to invest and the growing desire to put a portion of their money savings into the creative role of risk-taking investment.

Some financial analysts, such as those who work for mutual funds and trust companies, directly recommend or make actual investment decisions. They invest the money of their share owners, or their clients' trust accounts, in accordance with their evaluations of various securities. Others—such as those working for investment advisory services—write weekly, monthly, or quarterly reports advising clients to buy, sell, or

O. GLENN SAXON, JR. is Consultant—Professional Investor Relations, General Electric Company, New York, New York.

hold certain securities. Still others, primarily those who work for brokerage firms, constitute research departments which provide, through the customer's man or securities salesman, background information and recommendations to customers on the desirability of investments in certain kinds of stock.

Thus the share owners and potential share owners of every company are greatly influenced by the opinions of financial analysts concerning the worth of the company's shares; in fact, their opinions help create the market price by influencing the specific investment decisions of potential buyers or sellers.

The primary role of professional investor relations is to provide the financial analyst with better, more factual, more accurate, and more representative information about the company, its management, its character, and its prospects than the average analyst is likely to have learned, even if he has followed as carefully as possible all the available published material. This definitely does *not* mean that financial analysts should be given "inside" information. But because a financial analyst may be making or recommending an investment decision that will affect several hundred, several thousand, or even several hundred thousand shares, he has a critical financial responsibility to his clients; and the better analysts will study companies in far greater detail than is possible for the average share owner. At the General Electric Company, it is a basic rule that the same question will always be answered in the same way, whether it comes from a financial analyst or any other share owner. This obviously means that in some cases more information will be given to a financial analyst than to the average share owner—but this is because the financial analyst thinks about the company more, studies its operations, and is in a position to ask more informed and penetrating questions.

For the guidance of the executive concerned, it would be well to set forth certain principles and practices to govern the company's professional investor relations. As an example of what might be included, here are the ground rules that we try to observe at General Electric:

1. We try to be completely straightforward. If a question is in an area we consider confidential, we simply tell the analyst so, but we constantly try to insure that information about our company is made public unless there is a good reason to keep it confidential.
2. We do not give out earnings estimates or forecasts. It is the analyst's role to do this type of predicting or estimating, if he so desires, basing his estimates on the information and facts he asks for.
3. We do not give out profit margins by groups or monthly figures.
4. We are not afraid to admit it when we are stumped by a question;

but if the question is legitimate, we research the answer and call the analyst back with the information.

5. When an analyst calls for the first time, we take 15 to 30 minutes to outline our management philosophy, our organization structure, and a few other key factors that are important to the development of a balanced understanding of the company.
6. We do not give analysts souvenirs or favors of any intrinsic value, nor do we pay their transportation or living costs when they visit us or any of our plants.
7. We will not approve or disapprove any written reports by analysts about the company, nor will we correct in any degree estimates about facts we consider confidential; however, we will help an analyst check facts or figures for accuracy if they have been publicly released.
8. We do not make mailings to all analysts, nor even to all electrical-manufacturing-industry analysts; but occasionally we may make special mailings to those analysts who call on us regularly.

# NEW APPROACHES TO SPECIAL EVENTS FOR ANALYSTS •

JOHN A. GEARHART

FINANCIAL ANALYSTS ARE GROWING in number, influence, professional stature, and degree of specialization and are at the same time becoming much more widely dispersed geographically. All of these factors tend to make increasingly complex the problems and opportunities of any company which truly wishes to have financial analysts and other members of the financial community understand more about the business, its goals, and its expectations. And these factors will broaden the approaches that the modern business must take if it wants to give the analysts sufficient exposure to the company and to various levels of its management so the analysts can judge for themselves the degree to which the goals and expectations are capable of realization.

There are now about 8,200 members of analysts' societies—more than double the membership in the early 1950's—and their societies are now in virtually every major financial center in this country. More important than the growth in numbers of analysts is the growth of their influence and professional stature in the financial community. Today, more than ever before, these analysts are the experts listened to by investment committees of banks, brokerage firms, advisory services, trust funds, insurance companies, and other institutions for advice in making investment decisions as to whether to buy, hold, or sell a company's stock.

To provide these firms with better information and to study today's many diversified and highly technologically oriented companies, these analysts increasingly must specialize in their investment research. This may

JOHN A. GEARHART is Specialist—Professional Investor Relations, General Electric Company, New York, New York.

mean that more analysts will be interested in any one company from the standpoint either of evaluating the overall company or its efforts in a single product line of the business.

Almost all modern businesses are active in trying to reach the analysts with adequate information on a continuing basis, and few companies now fail to recognize the importance of the analysts as a vital link to their present and potential share owners. The need, then, is to consider carefully the variety of approaches open to a company to widen and improve its information flow to analysts and to gain from each of these approaches the maximum benefit for the company.

In general, a program for communicating about a company rests upon a person-to-person approach with analysts. The alert company, of course, personally and regularly reaches those analysts most important to it, and it will supplement these personal contacts with special events which add content and dimension to an analyst's understanding of the business. The company provides these special events not as an on-again, off-again activity but as a regular part of its total program of investor relations.

There are a number of paths open to the company which really recognizes the importance of this work and sets about to develop new approaches:

1. Field management visits for large groups of analysts.
2. Field management visits for selected groups of analysts.
3. Management appearances before analysts' conventions, society meetings, and specialized analysts' groups.
4. Analysts' attendance at the annual meeting of share owners.

Each of these approaches in one way or another provides a different platform for presenting a distinct type of information about the business and its management. The sophisticated analyst will look to each of these special events for what it will contribute to his understanding of the competitive spirit motivating the company, its prospects, and the ability of management at various levels to bring the company to its goals.

### FIELD MANAGEMENT VISITS FOR LARGE GROUPS

The time when analysts wanted to visit a plant to take a few days off on a junket—if there ever were such a day—faded long ago. The growth of security analysis as a profession and the recognition by management of the importance of communicating to analysts have put real value into these visits.

Today the plant visit is a visit to talk with the management at the operating levels. On these visits, analysts observe the quality of operating management, the scope of its responsibilities, and the authority and freedom available to managers in making key decisions in their business areas.

The opportunity to provide these trips often arises in connection with analysts' conventions and their regional conferences. In these cases, the group visiting a facility may number anywhere from 50 to 250. For these large groups, formal management presentations tend to be a necessity. There are definite advantages to this in that a great deal of background preparation must take place and a well-planned schedule of activities must be worked out to include management presentations, a question-and-answer period, and a tour of the facilities. Careful attention to these matters is, of course, important with a group of any size that is visiting a plant facility, but with the larger groups, time and number of people involved dictate more precise planning.

To make the visit effective for the analysts, key operating management should be on hand to make presentations and to answer questions. In my experience with management presentations at various General Electric locations, I have found that there are at least three basic things that make up a good presentation: (1) some discussion of the background or history of the operation; (2) a general look at the resources involved; and (3) as thorough a consideration as is possible of the total market and a general discussion of those areas of the market currently attractive to the business. Presenting this information to analysts will give them far greater understanding of the business than they had before a visit. One helpful way to think of these presentations is that the analysts' interests and viewpoints are not too dissimilar to those of the company's board of directors, although, of course, for competitive reasons management will be far more limited in what it can or should say to the analysts as compared with directors.

If one function of the business such as marketing, engineering, manufacturing, or research is especially important to the long-range development of the business, management should try to place the proper amount of emphasis on that function. Analysts recognize that this varies from business to business, and they will profit from the type of information presented to them.

Some analysts often feel they do not have an accurate picture of a business unless operating statistics such as sales and profits by product lines or dollars invested in the business are spelled out. However, it is quite possible to add substantially to analysts' understanding of a business without being specific about this type of information. Analysts, who must spend their time looking at a number of companies, have only a limited amount of information about what takes place in a department of any one business; yet a company usually seeks the opportunity to communicate far more than this fraction of information to those sincerely interested in a particular phase of the business. A company can do an adequate job of informing the analysts if it will answer legitimate questions while avoiding the relatively small amount which, if given, would be competitively detrimental to the business or otherwise improper to release to a select few.

There are few manufacturing, engineering, or research operations worth the time of analysts which are simple enough to explain effectively and in a relatively short period of time to a large number of analysts. Thus it is important that small groups of analysts at any one time be taken through your facilities—groups numbering, say, less than ten. Nothing is more ludicrous than seeing analysts standing ten deep, peering over one another's shoulders, and cupping their ears to hear an explanation of an automated assembly line or some advanced engineering development through the din of regular plant operations.

The proper approach to a tour through the plant depends not only on the size of the group but also on the individual assigned to conduct it. Not only should this person be a good speaker, but he should have two other qualities: he should be enough of a specialist to know in detail the function he is describing and be broad enough in his outlook to provide a reasonable understanding of where the function fits in the total operation.

Several other factors can help make the plant tour a good one. For example, it can be made more understandable by displaying and explaining a layout of the plant before the tour; or if there is a film of the plant's operations, it can be similarly used. If a special process in the plant lends itself to a blackboard explanation, this too can be discussed in advance and will result in a more interested group viewing the actual process.

With this kind of preparation, the plant tour won't simply be a hike for the health of those taking part, but rather it can blend in with what the analysts have heard in the management presentations. It can provide a valuable extra dimension to the information analysts take away with them because the overall efficiency of operations, modern equipment, and the attitude of plant personnel will not be lost on the perceptive analyst.

### VISITS FOR SELECTED GROUPS OF ANALYSTS

One of the continuing efforts at General Electric is to provide periodic trips to operating locations for small, selected groups of analysts. Usually less than ten analysts at a time make these trips, and we try to invite those who have indicated a high degree of interest in an operation and who have relatively the same background experience. A mutual respect among the analysts makes for a better trip because they will contribute importantly to one another's viewpoints, and a far greater amount of worthwhile information will develop in the question-and-answer sessions with management.

Not only does this type of visit develop a better understanding of the business, but it makes the optimum use of the time of both operating management and the analysts. Usually the job can best be done by setting aside a full day for the analysts' visit; in this way management can devote the proper amount of attention to the visit, and it will result in all activities—management presentations, question-and answer periods, and a tour of the facilities—taking on a more meaningful perspective. Analysts, too, will have profitably spent their time and will leave a plant with a far better understanding of its operations.

It is likely that there are less than 50 to 100 analysts—and not all of them are necessarily members of societies—who follow a company regularly and therefore become fully grounded in its history, its business areas, and its methods of operating. These are the analysts most important to the company and with whom management visits are most useful because they are based upon background understanding built up over time.

In these days when many companies have a high degree of diversification, certain departments of a company come into special prominence from time to time with the investment community. Analysts who have never or rarely been in touch with a company will begin to contact it regularly. A case in point for General Electric was the ground swell of interest in the atomic power business during late 1962 and early 1963. However, for at least two years prior to this, selected groups of analysts visited with the management of the atomic power equipment business and, I think, gained a great deal of background understanding which was important to the company during the upswing of interest in this business.

We do not encourage analysts to visit one of the company's locations by paying their travel or living expenses on a trip, but rather we believe their basic interest in knowing more about an operation should determine whether they make the trip. Once at the operating facility, we try to be good hosts, but we do not give them any souvenirs or favors of any intrinsic value. Investment analysts expect to be treated as professionals, and professional treatment involves a proper approach to matters sometimes seemingly incidental or trivial.

### APPEARANCES BEFORE ANALYSTS' SOCIETIES AND OTHER GROUPS

Perhaps the oldest and best-known approach to talking with analysts is the periodic appearances of management before societies of analysts. The growth in the number of these societies means that opportunities for management to appear before various groups of analysts are becoming more and more numerous. In addition to the large metropolitan societies, requests for management presentations may come from the newer societies in young but growing financial centers or in connection with conventions and regional conferences of analysts. Invitations are also frequently received from the smaller, more specialized groups of analysts who concentrate on certain industries or segments of industries.

It is only natural for all of these societies and groups to ask for the chief executive officer, the chairman of the board, or a top officer to appear before their members; but the time of these executives is limited, and they simply cannot fill all of the requests they receive. We have tried to fill this need by talking further with the representatives of the societies to find out if there is not some business area of the company, such as electronics components or atomic power, which is of special or current interest to their members. In this way, the company's top experts in a particular product area give them far more understanding of that business than would otherwise be possible. And over a period of time and with a number of appearances, this information subsequently broadens out to a great number of analysts.

Here, too, analysts see and hear the men who now are in positions which may lead them to the top executive levels some years hence. These are also the men whose important decisions today may vitally affect what businesses a company may be a major participant in later on. In a number of instances after these appearances, analysts have pointed out how effective this type of presentation has been for them and how it adds to their understanding of the company's total efforts.

At the same time, the experience of appearing before analysts' societies has proved to be very desirable to operating people who otherwise have little exposure to the financial community and its interests. Many of these men operate businesses comparable in scope to those of competitors' whose officers normally appear before such groups. In these appearances, operating managers limit their presentations to their product areas but generally cover the same topics as their counterparts in other companies.

### ANALYSTS AT THE ANNUAL MEETING

The annual meeting of share owners is another opportunity—often overlooked in the past—to broaden constructive relationships with financial analysts. Here is the once-a-year occasion when top management and the board of directors are on hand to report on the business to its owners.

Presenting general business and economic information as a regular part of the meeting provides the analysts with a different type of information than is available through the field visit or even the management appearances before various analysts' groups. The information developed in the general discussion period will probably be more fundamental to the growth of the business and more long range in nature. For example, the questions asked by analysts at General Electric's 1963 annual meeting concerned such matters as price trends, the Apollo contract, taxes, and the Common Market.

From another standpoint, analysts' attendance at annual meetings can be of great significance in future years. The question of how analysts go about following the companies they study is already of increasing interest. The annual meeting is an opportunity for the analysts—who should be the most professional judges of management's abilities—to see and observe management, to hear reports of the business, and to ask questions they consider important to making their evaluations. This can be an occasion for analysts to gain further understanding of the ability, foresight, and character of management—an evaluation most critical to the analysts' work.

## A PROFESSIONAL APPROACH

The wide variety of opportunities available to a company to improve its relations with financial analysts puts special emphasis on developing a complete and continuing program. Each activity of this effort can contribute to the effectiveness of the total program and can mean better, more efficient utilization of company resources in this direction. If a continuing program is established, it will help assure a more personalized and direct means of communicating to analysts. It will mean a continual flow of information—of specific usefulness and in the proper perspective—to the sophisticated financial analysts' community.

Moreover, the ultimate purpose of communicating to analysts centers on continually providing accurate information so that informed buyers and sellers in the market can determine realistic and fair stock prices. This, in turn, helps fulfill what every management responsible to its share owners desires—a reasonable market appraisal of the worth of the share owners' investment in the company.

# SECTION V

## *Completing the Task*

*Once a program of investor relations is in operation, the job must be completed in a number of ways. Research and analysis of the program's various elements play a vital role in adapting it to changing conditions. Even the largest corporation may occasionally need outside help in conducting a full program. Moreover, management must see to it that the highest ethical standards are maintained. The company has a responsibility to promote the greater economic education of investors. Most of all, in pursuit of one of the primary goals of investor relations, the company should exert every effort to broaden share ownership.*

# RESEARCH TECHNIQUES IN INVESTOR RELATIONS •

RAYMOND J. DODGE

WITH THE EXPLOSIVE GROWTH of share ownership in the last ten years, corporations have been more than ever focusing their attention on their share owners—trying new ways to supply them with information, looking for methods of stimulating their interest, actively soliciting their views, and encouraging their constructive participation. Generally speaking, however, this growing interest in share owners, the ambitious plans for improved share owner programs, and the various activities designed to broaden stock ownership are all going forward with very little reliable information about the characteristics and opinions of the people who own stock.

In this scientific age, it has become almost axiomatic that the chances of success in many fields—marketing, employee relations, politics—are greatly increased by the use of research to obtain knowledge about the characteristics and opinions of customers, employees, or voters. Share ownership, however, is an area that has not yet seen the application of any great amount of research. It is remarkable that so many companies have over the years put money and effort into their investor relations programs with little or no attempt to analyze the audience or measure the results. This is even more surprising in view of the importance of the share owners to the business—as owners who are the basic source of authority and capital and also as customers and ambassadors for its products, as suppliers of new capital, and as ready and vocal supporters of efforts to achieve a better economic and political climate in which to operate.

---

RAYMOND J. DODGE is Consultant—Investor Research and Data Analysis, General Electric Company, New York, New York.

Of course, there is some background information to be found in the 1952 Brookings Institution study, surveys by the New York Stock Exchange, and studies by the National Bureau of Economic Research, the Federal Reserve System, and the Internal Revenue Service. But for practical application to individual problems, a company needs specific information about its own share owners in order to point the direction of its investor relations program and enable it to make more effective use of the money it spends on share owner relations.

In recent years an increasing number of companies large and small have been making a start toward obtaining more information about their share owners. Most of my illustrations will be taken from the General Electric research program because I am most familiar with it. But such companies as AT&T, Arvin, DuPont, Ford, IBM, Joy Manufacturing, Pitney-Bowes, Southern Company, Standard Oil of New Jersey, Union Carbide, and U.S. Steel have all done sound work in share owner research. Undoubtedly this is not a complete list. Understandably a company which puts effort into an important project is reluctant to give away its competitive advantages by broadly publicizing its findings. Quite properly too there is an underlying feeling that the share owner-company relationship is a confidential one. So it may well be that the amount of current research in share ownership is larger than is generally known.

### THE WILLINGNESS OF SHARE OWNERS TO COOPERATE

Probably one of the most notable discoveries that any company will make in its first share owner research work is the willingness—even eagerness—of the share owners to cooperate. Experience shows that the size of the response to a survey, the number of questions that can be covered, and the depth of "sensitive" information that can be obtained have all far exceeded the estimates of survey experts. Some of this is the result, of course, of the special relationship the share owner feels toward his company. But there is some indication that share owners have a desire for participation, for identification, for recognition; and often a survey is the first contact by the company that meets these needs.

This means that any of the usual research techniques can be used—mail and telephone surveys, personal interviews, group discussions, and so forth—without the need for any special incentive to encourage response. The results can probably be expected to be more satisfactory than if the same survey were directed at the general public. In fact, the main problem is likely to be a natural bias toward being too helpful, too favorable, too ready to gloss over criticism.

## RESEARCH IN THE RECORDS

Before turning to the survey methods which can be used in acquiring information *from* share owners, it is important to consider some of the information *about* share owners which can be obtained by internal research work without making any survey at all. To begin with, the basic records will yield quite a bit of useful information. The following is a representative list:

1. Number of share owners, divided into groups according to the number of shares owned. This gives a picture of the share owners as people who are available to read company communications, buy its products, and lend their support in controversies affecting the business.
2. Number of shares, divided into groups according to size of holdings. This shows the source of voting strength at the annual meetings and the ready potential market for the sale of new securities.
3. Geographic distribution. This will tell us if the local citizens in the communities where we operate have a stake in the company which can help us gain their understanding and support if necessary.
4. Types of owners. A very high percentage of stock held in institutional names may sometimes be a danger signal; but aside from that, a company will have to work through the various financial intermediaries when it wants to communicate with the underlying or beneficial owners of stock.
5. Stability of the share owner list. This will indicate if we can plan a continuing communications program aimed largely at the same people over a long period of time.

## OTHER INTERNAL ANALYSES

Proxy voting is another area where internal analysis may well pay off. Of course, the record of total shares and accounts voted and the percentage voted in support of management show the broad results of the proxy-solicitation effort. But a more detailed analysis by size and type of holding, for example, may help to evaluate different elements of the solicitation program against the cost of each. Study of the source of votes "for" as well as "against" specific proposals may indicate the need for a future communications program or give some measure of the effectiveness of one already undertaken.

A careful analysis of the tone and substance of correspondence received from share owners may be a qualitative measure of the share owner program or an indicator of communications needs. Particularly before the annual meeting, this can suggest questions that may arise and thus serve to have the chairman fully prepared to answer them.

Certainly a listed company should keep a systematic watch on the short- and long-term market action of its stock as a measure of investor opinion. The frequency and accuracy of information about the company given in advisory services, market letters, and security analysts' reports is some indication of the success of communication with the financial community. But the ultimate financial measure of an investor relations program is the price level of the company's stock in comparison with that of other companies that make up the competition in the industry and in the financial markets. Of course, this does not mean a high price level per se but rather a realistic price level based on relative performance and prospects.

## MAIL AND TELEPHONE SURVEYS

A mail survey is probably the simplest and least expensive method of obtaining information from share owners. This technique also lends itself to a wide variety of treatment to fit a particular circumstance. A return postcard with a few questions might be included with the annual report or some other publication or given to those who attend the annual meeting. Or a much more elaborate questionnaire might be mailed with a letter of explanation and return envelope to all the share owners or to a selected group of them.

One shortcoming of mail surveys, of course, is that we have no knowledge about those who fail to reply. Theoretically, the response may come more heavily from one group than from another—men rather than women, older people rather than younger, the favorably inclined rather than the critics, or vice versa—so we cannot be sure whether there is a distortion in the results or in which direction it goes. Fortunately in the share owner relations area there are several elements which let mail surveys work out better than they might otherwise.

For several years we have been mailing a four-page questionnaire to the share owners who attend the annual meeting to get their overall reactions as well as their impressions of individual parts of the program. Normally the response has run about 60 per cent or better, which is so much higher than the response to the average mail survey that the likelihood of any strong bias is greatly reduced. Furthermore, when the surveys include some questions which can be checked against the registrations or other information—number of shares owned, home address, sex, employee or nonemployee—the respondents always seem to be remarkably representative in this regard. In addition, the range of comment is great enough for us to be sure that both critics and admirers are heard from.

The most important consideration, however, in this kind of work is recognizing that it is the trends which really matter more than the absolute figures. Whether 50 per cent or 75 per cent of the audience liked some particular item on the agenda is not as important as whether the change made this year improved the audience reaction as compared to last year. Therefore, there should be no hesitancy about using the mail-survey technique in the proper circumstances because it can give very satisfactory results at a very low cost.

In other cases a telephone survey may meet a particular need. After one large plant had experimentally carried on a communications program with some of the share owners in the local community area, an appraisal of the program was quickly yet thoroughly developed from telephone calls to share owners who had been receiving the material and to others who had not.

Joy Manufacturing has used the telephone interview technique for a much broader national survey of its share owners. General Electric has also used it to determine the share owners' "recall" of the report of our annual meeting. In these cases, the interviewing was done by an outside firm with strategically located people who had previous experience in talking with share owners.

## SURVEYS THROUGH PERSONAL INTERVIEWS

Because the annual report is the most important and usually the most expensive single item in a share owner relations program, its readership should be measured with special care to insure a high degree of validity. This will probably require engaging a firm that specializes in this kind of work to conduct a personal-interview survey.

Ten of the past eleven General Electric annual reports have been studied in surveys of this type, which proved to be well worth their cost by making it possible to improve the readership of the report. As a result of detailed readership data, features that had been traditional were dropped for lack of interest, features that were considered too long were shortened, items of special interest were amplified, and new features were added. The company has also been able to tailor the less-read features of the report more closely to the readers' interests.

In personal interviews it is often possible to ask an extra question or two which goes beyond the readership of the publication into the area of share owner attitudes. Some time ago, for example, when the share owners were asked what they thought about the company's speaking out on public affairs in general, they indicated that they felt the company should speak out on legislation affecting the company, state its views on national issues as they affect the company, and urge people to vote; but (not surprisingly) they agreed that the company should not back specific candidates for public office.

This attitude led to devoting part of the share owner communications program to discussion of such matters as inflation, productivity and national economic growth, capital formation, and many others. It also resulted in an experiment in which several plants have been furnished with lists of share owners in their local communities for use in special local communications programs or other activities where share owner interest and support can be a help to them.

As a part of another personal-interview survey, share owners were asked how and when they acquired the electrical appliances in their homes, and the brands were noted. Among those who bought each of the seven appliances tested, the proportion of share owners who selected the General Electric brand was markedly higher than the proportion of the general public who had done so—in some cases, as much as two and a half times as high.

This product loyalty has encouraged some steps in the direction of selling to share owners, for example, by mailing to them a specially prepared, comprehensive catalog of appliances and other consumer products. Furthermore, each new share owner receives, along with his welcome letter, a form that lists appliances and other types of products for home use. Besides informing him of the wide variety of our consumer products, the form can be used to obtain information about any of these products in which he has particular interest.

Personal interviews with share owners have been used to good advantage by such companies as AT&T, Keystone Steel and Wire, and Western Union. In a regular program, employees visit substantial numbers of individual share owners, usually in their homes, to discuss company affairs and answer questions that may be of concern to the share owners. These visits are not aimed at obtaining a statistical analysis of the share owner body, but they provide a great deal of useful information about share owner attitudes, opinions, and problems.

### SUCCESS WITH DISCUSSION GROUPS

Another technique that can be used profitably in cases where statistical analysis is not required is the roundtable discussion. Several times, in one or another of the larger cities, we have asked five or six of the local security analysts who actively follow General Electric to make a critical review of the annual report. The resulting discussion of their ideas about it usually lasts three hours or so. The analysts always give a good deal of thought to the report in advance and shower us with sound, thoughtful comments and suggestions. Some of these ideas can be put into effect at once, and some naturally must be put aside for consideration in the future—but they are all worthwhile.

In 1963 the same idea was tried out experimentally with individual share owners. Four discussion groups, averaging about five share owners per group, were led first into general discussion of the annual report as a whole and then into reactions to the individual features of the report. Each discussion lasted about two hours: naturally there were many different points of view, particularly about specific details, but there were also some common threads of comment running through the discussions which will be considered very carefully when planning the next annual report. In this case, also, no statistical analysis is possible, but the discussions certainly humanized the cold figures of the readership survey.

### THE ROLE OF LONG-RANGE RESEARCH

In addition, broader, long-range research into the characteristics, attitudes, and motivations of share owners is necessary if the company wants to improve its relationships with its share owners.

For the longer run, too, the problem of broadening stock ownership is a challenging one. Even with the record-breaking total of 17 million share owners, the ownership of stock is still far less popular than other types of investment such as life insurance, savings bonds, and bank accounts. This is an area in which research is greatly needed, for we do not know what the barriers to share ownership really are. What are the thresholds of income, wealth, knowledge, and perhaps political outlook that people must cross before they buy shares in United States corporations?

General Electric has completed one major project in this long-range area: an extensive study of nonemployee individuals who own stock in their own names. With the help of outside consultants, a "national probability sample" of 155 counties was selected from the more than 3,000 counties in the United States. The accuracy of this sample proved out by projecting the national figures for retail sales, United States savings bond sales, bank deposits, population, and other economic and social characteristics within a margin no greater than plus or minus 2 per cent. Next, a random sample of about 40,000 General Electric share owners was selected as a national cross section, and statisticians selected from among these a group of 3,000 whose addresses were in the counties that comprised the probability sample. These share owners were interviewed by an outside research organization, after the interviewers were tested and approved by the company.

The questionnaire, designed with the help of outside consultants, consisted of 11 pages and more than a hundred questions, more than half of which were open end. Hardly any of the share owners objected to the lengthy interviews, which averaged almost two hours, and many treated the interview almost as a social occasion.

The share owners were surprisingly willing to provide detailed financial data about their income and wealth situations. Furthermore, a great deal of information was obtained about their economic attitudes, their relations with and interest in the company, their investment practices and objectives, and the role of the company's stock in their financial planning.

The results of this research have been most helpful in developing programs for the future, defining the share owner frame of reference in which the company operates, and helping management to understand the dimensions of the problems that will be faced in the years ahead.

* * *

There may have been a time when a company could take the position that a share owner who didn't like the way the company was run could sell his stock, but today that attitude has all but disappeared. Share owners are growing in number and influence. They are taking a long-term savings approach to stock ownership, and they are showing more interest and desire to participate in the affairs of their companies.

Among other things, this means that we must have better annual meetings, better publications, and better understanding of share owners at all levels of management. Research in stock ownership is necessary to provide for these needs of today as well as for the opportunities of the future. Companies must find out how they can best develop the greatest untapped resource that business has: a body of share owners ready, willing, and able to supply the tremendous amounts of capital that business is going to need—people whose self-interest will make them eager participants in and vocal supporters of the private enterprise system.

# THE ROLE OF OUTSIDE CONSULTANTS IN INVESTOR RELATIONS •

WILLIAM E. CHATLOS

---

THE ROLE OF OUTSIDE CONSULTANTS in investor relations is basically one of providing perspective. To justify their economic existence, consultants must have the capacity to provide more and better services at less cost than a company would have to incur for the additional personnel and facilities for an internal corporate staff to provide the same services. There are a few unpleasant exceptions to this rule.

The use of outside consultants in investor relations in recent years is in large part a reflection of the shortage of readily available competent personnel. The entire field of investor relations has had such a quick growth that the philosophy and ground rules for sound decision making have not as yet reached a stage of easy codification. It is difficult to teach investor relations to others when the teachers are experiencing a constant re-evaluation of current procedures.

As might be anticipated, there is great variety in the services offered by outside consultants in this field. Any discussion of this subject is therefore a matter of individual interpretation. The strengths and selling points of some consultants are openly questioned by others—not only on grounds of effectiveness and propriety but also on the basis of ethics. In a field as dynamic and expanding as investor relations, it is obviously difficult to examine closely or justify the procedures and recommendations of the extreme elements. However, there are certain patterns and considerations that are common to all, and it is in this area that we can profitably examine the role of outside consultants.

---

WILLIAM E. CHATLOS is Principal, Georgeson & Co., New York, New York.

GENERAL PATTERNS AND CONSIDERATIONS

The specific needs of a company will indicate how often or even whether an outside consultant is necessary or desirable. In numerous instances a corporate staff may be adequately performing its duties under an existing program, but an unforeseen need may arise. A company may need a special booklet for analysts or an analysis and interpretation of stockholder data. It may have an unusually high percentage of broker or nominee holdings, feel the need for an outside review of corporate procedures, or desire some new ideas on how to cope with a disruptive annual meeting. Other important areas may demand attention from a staff that may not have the time to handle the situation properly. In these instances, the outside consultant may be the best solution.

The professional consultant works with a variety of companies and is exposed to many ideas. The better consultants are constantly looking for new approaches to handling a problem. The ideas which the consultant brings to an inside staff are sometimes not readily available to the company. A corporate program which relies solely on internal creativity and ideas may sometimes become stale over a period of time.

A company using a consultant has a right to expect both objectivity and perspective, which are particularly important in the field of investor relations. Public relations habits and techniques superimposed on corporate communications to stockholders and security analysts can have disastrous consequences. Objectivity is essential to the attainment of a fair market price. A shading of the truth in any direction may eventually come to be regarded as a subtle fraud by the financial community and stockholders.

Few tears are shed for the company or organization which deliberately misleads the investing public and subsequently gets what it deserves in the marketplace. The true tragedy occurs when an honest and well-meaning person in the company simply lets his optimism, enthusiasm, and fond wishes color his presentation. The financial community has a long memory when it finds it has been misled, even when this is unintentional.

Security analysts have a way of probing and searching for attractive elements in a situation, and at times companies permit the analysts to carry away a mistaken impression or innocently tell analysts what they think the analysts want to hear. The company that is subsequently found guilty of such practices will find it agonizingly difficult to work itself back into the confidence and good graces of the financial community. The reconstruction period may well run as long as a decade.

A consultant who is well informed on the affairs of the company can, in situations like these, render an incalculable service to his client not only by giving advice but also by helping to sift the management presentation to eliminate the froth and leave only the facts. He must counsel against the glamorous boast that makes good copy for analysts and stockholders over the short term. In some cases, the consultant is able to make more objective critiques of top management's presentations.

A conscientious consultant not only should not hesitate to insist on objectivity in the best interests of his client but recognizes that it is a special responsibility to which he must devote his attention. A consultant-client relationship is of necessity a highly personal one. The consultant may find that he has to establish a rapport to determine what the president really thinks of a given situation and then base his recommendation partly on his subjective evaluation of the president. All analysts are familiar with the conservative president to whom they listen carefully and then add 10 per cent to whatever estimates are given. The reverse is true with the overly optimistic president. Here the judgment of the consultant in recommending procedures is of tantamount importance, and yet this is an area that is most difficult to measure in determining the value of the consultant.

Most good consultants in this field can recall many instances of trying to convince some managements to reduce optimistic estimates of earnings as well as to persuade others to adopt a more realistic approach in estimating future earnings. The built-in preferences of management are difficult to change. An outside viewpoint, particularly if it has been bolstered by a past record of sound advice, can be a healthy sounding board and a means to fruitful discussion. It has often been said that the job at the top is a lonely and difficult one, and a major reason for this is that the chief executive is already at the top of the ladder and therefore has few sources from which he can appropriately seek advice. A qualified consultant can sometimes provide an excellent answer to this problem.

The consultant should have a sense of perspective. He must be able to visualize all of the elements and design a program to mesh the more desirable current activities with the new ideas and innovations that are necessary to achieve the program objectives. At the same time, most corporations will insist that the changes be effected with a smooth continuity. Abrupt changes or breaks in policy or past performance should be generally avoided.

At this point a word of caution may be in order. The outside consultant must also know when to say "I don't know." In some cases, a consultant may be hired to talk with analysts on behalf of a company. If he talks with analysts or the press, the consultant acts in the capacity of an agent of the company, and his actions will have a direct bearing on the success of its program. A consultant who encourages others to think he is an expert in all aspects of a client's operations is risking the success of the client's program. An analyst has a right to be distinctly annoyed with a consultant —or anyone else for that matter—who somehow feels it beneath his dignity or construes it as a sign of weakness to admit that he lacks an answer.

The consultant needs to be a reasonably informed but not necessarily an "expert" representative of the company. There will be many areas of inquiry in which the consultant should be sufficiently astute to realize his ignorance of the subject and ask for information from a specialist within the company. In any given discussion with an informed analyst, the point will be rather quickly reached when the consultant should arrange to obtain specific information from an expert source or to arrange an interview for the analyst with the individual most able to provide accurate information. In this event, the consultant may best act as a counselor to the persons in the company who should directly interview the analysts.

When an analyst is doing a detailed study, the consultant should insist that the analyst talk directly with the company. In making a study of a company, analysts will want to talk to management for two reasons. First, management is obviously closer to the company's activities than is the consultant; but, second, talking with management gives the analysts a chance to evaluate the officers, which has an important bearing on the conclusions reached. When an outside consultant works with analysts on behalf of a company, his job is to keep the analysts abreast of current information and avoid unnecessary calls to management on questions which he can answer easily.

## PROGRAM OBJECTIVES AND THE CONSULTANT

The topics covered in most chapters in this book could be handled by some outside consultant with special emphasis given to the subject from the particular viewpoint of the individual consultant. Recommendations of outside consultants on any given aspect of this field are to some extent dependent on the background of the individual consultant. The advertising agency that enters the investor relations field will understandably tend to devote a large part of its recommended program to advertising. The client that hires a publicity firm may find that publicity and "column inches" occupy a disproportionate part of the program. A firm that has a reputation of "moving prices" exhibits a tendency to operate in quite a different way from the firm that sells its services on the basis of its expertness in public relations or in communications skills.

A careful review of the services offered by a number of consultant firms will usually reveal a basic pattern which characterizes the methods employed by the firm. These are generally the result of many years' experience in handling a variety of assignments. The unique or highly successful solutions employed by the consultants contribute to and form the basis of the reputation of the consultant. Success in certain areas leads to referrals and recommendations and attracts new clients who desire similar services. The consultant may thus offer a wide range of services, but in reality his reputation is usually dependent on a specialty which probably lies in the successful application of investor relations principles to rather closely defined sets of circumstances.

The company which is considering the use of outside consultants must pay attention to the factor of specialization if satisfactory results are to be obtained. If the corporation seeks a "package" deal in which community relations, advertising, public relations, and investor relations are to be included under the same contract, firms which specialize in any one of these four areas would obviously be eliminated, although the specialists may have the most to offer in a specific situation. On the other hand, if a company is interested only in financial publicity, for example, the wise thing would be to seek a firm which has established a reputation in that field.

One type of role played by consultants is a servicing role. Outside consultants are usually asked to provide a *complete* service in the investor relations field for a small or medium-sized company where the internal public relations staff consists of one person or where there is no such staff. In this situation the consultant's job extends from the highest policy-making level to the most menial of chores and involves an almost daily working relationship with the client. Programs must be originated and implemented. The role of the consultant in this case is roughly equivalent to that of a large staff in a major corporation.

Essentially, the consultant's job will be divided into two areas: working with the inside staff and implementing the company's program on his own. In the former case, the consultant will offer guidance and sit in on policy meetings in order to give the benefit of his experience. The consultant will also play a major role in the decisions concerning the production of printed material. However, considering the additional research that a consultant must do in gathering material for producing financial statements for stockholders and analysts, it is normally more economical for the company to have its own staff do as much of this as possible.

Problems will arise when management does not draw a distinct line between the responsibilities of the permanent staff and the consultant. The staff may feel the consultant should be doing more work than the consultant had originally understood he was to do. The company's employees may take the opportunity to try to lighten some of their workload. On the other hand, the consultant may try to absorb some of the functions of the staff. Any one of these situations results in friction and can hamper the consultant's efforts. Instead of working together, the two groups may be competing for assignments or avoiding responsibilities. Most good consultants have experienced these situations at one time or another. However, if sharp lines of responsibility are clearly drawn at the beginning, these problems can be avoided.

As a policy matter, my firm prefers to limit participation and activities to those areas not readily handled by the inside staff. This provides a natural dividing line which eliminates the routine servicing from the consultant's province and involves him in those activities where his special knowledge is most useful.

A second type of role is where the consultant acts in a consulting capacity with little or no servicing required. Variations in the role of the consultant are generally related to the size of the company. Medium-sized companies are usually capable of utilizing their own staffs for most routine activities. Companies located at some distance from the financial markets may require assistance in servicing the press in the major metropolitan areas or in having the consultant act as the corporate representative and liaison with Wall Street. This arrangement seems to be most attractive to many corporations and outside consultants. In our own experience, this role has become increasingly important in recent years.

At the present time, larger companies are among those most aware of the advantages of using the special skills of outside consultants, either on a permanent basis or for specific assignments. The increased complexity of investor relations has made it virtually impossible for even the largest corporation to be wholly on its own.

Naturally enough, the consultant handles more sophisticated projects in the large company. Research procedures and interpretation, readability studies, program planning, and specific projects occupy much of his time. In addition, consultants can sometimes pinch-hit for corporate staffs on special tasks such as analyzing the unusual and providing information on subjects which may arise on only rare occasions. Because the consultant is subjected to a wide variety of experiences, many smaller companies retain consultants for such specific questions. The latter is more akin to a retainer arrangement than full consulting. Usually the amount of consulting required is minimal, and the fees are modest.

A third role of the consultant combines the features of the servicing relationship with the middle-sized corporation and the consulting activities with the larger companies. This role might be termed that of troubleshooter.

Because of the inherently critical nature of certain problems, the advice, counsel, and servicing of the outside consultant are practically mandatory. Trouble situations usually have a time factor that dictates urgency and speed.

A number of years ago we were asked to review the stockholder records of a company that was curious about the reasons for an unusually heavy volume of trading. A careful study revealed a very sizable accumulation of stock by a group of new stockholders, and defensive measures were undertaken. Procedures were established to provide quick and complete information regarding trading patterns, and at the same time a simultaneous study and analysis was made of the stockholder list. Shortly thereafter a plan was set in motion to acquire stock to counteract the purchases. Major stockholders were contacted, and discussions with the opposition were initiated. The measures taken in this situation were completely new to the company officers and staff.

In contrast to this emergency program was the long-range approach which was designed to solve the problem of a company with 45 per cent of its stock in street name. This problem is a most uncommon one. In this case programing and analysis are more important than time. Few corporate staffs either face or resolve this type of problem in a lifetime, although as outside consultants we had experienced similar situations a number of times.

It certainly can be stated that for the servicing of most investor relations programs, the functions of a competent internal staff are on a par with those of an outside consultant. For this reason, we have not dealt in this paper with the specific details of servicing done by consultants which would be comparable to the servicing provided by an existing internal staff. Our initial contention was that the basic role of consultants was to provide that which was not readily available from an internal staff. In the absence of internal staff, the outside consultant should be used to initiate the corporate program and plan for the eventual installation of an internal staff.

## STEPS IN HIRING A CONSULTANT

The first step in hiring a consultant does not involve a consultant at all! The company must decide beforehand what it wants. This is not as simple as it sounds. Probably the greatest single reason for dissatisfaction with investor relations programs involving outside consultants is that the company did not know what it wanted in the first place.

Basic considerations are in order here. Benjamin Graham, the dean of security analysts, has stated that all of a company's activities in behalf of its stockholders are eventually reflected in the market price and dividends. A stockholder has a right to buy and sell at a fair price. An objective and candid study of the corporate situation should clearly define the investor relations goals and make it relatively easy to decide on an outside consultant.

It must be noted here that some managements help keep the relatively few incompetent consultants in business by ignoring the proper procedures in hiring a consultant. In addition, some few managements unfortunately employ unscrupulous consultants who use methods that management would not condone in its own staffs. In both cases, the end result over a long period of time will prove to be highly unsatisfactory.

Moreover, the company should interview more than one consulting firm. Management should feel free to ask any questions which it thinks pertinent, for specific examples of work done for other companies, and for the background and previous experience of the consulting firm. It should review a list of the consulting firm's clients. A professional consulting firm will normally invite the prospective client to check with current and past clients. Finally, a company should match the consultant's strengths with the program goals.

The company should come to the consulting firm with a specific idea of its needs, although this may be revised after discussion, and should ask the consultant how similar problems were resolved. It is also important that an acceptable personal relationship be established. It is wise to investigate the firm's ethics: because of the confidential nature of the relationship, the ethical standards of the firm must be beyond question.

Before the final move is made to hire a consulting firm, a company should check references from banks, law firms, and financial sources. Finally, it should make sure that the areas of responsibility between the company and the consultant are clearly defined in the contract.

# ETHICAL CONSIDERATIONS IN INVESTOR RELATIONS •

JOHN F. CHILDS

COMMENTS IN THE OTHER CHAPTERS of this book have covered most of what can be said about ethical considerations, since almost every facet of investor relations calls for attention to what is ethically right and wrong. However, we hope in this chapter to bring together in one place the various aspects of this subject.

Investors are, of course, directly interested in security prices; but what is perhaps more important is the fact that security markets play a major part in our national economy. That economy benefits from a smooth flow of capital into the right fields, and the security markets tend to direct the flow of savings, particularly when full information is made broadly available to investors. Laws and regulations help prevent or correct abuses in and encourage disclosure of information about the company that is important to investors. But in the last analysis it is management which in its own good conscience and enlightened self-interest must carry out its obligations with the highest motives in order for our capitalistic economy to function efficiently.

In order for management to do its part there are two prerequisites. First, management must constantly be mindful of its proper role, that of working for the stockholders. This awareness is the best assurance that management will understand all the ethical considerations of its position, including those which concern its relations to investors. Second, management must be aware of the proper purpose of an investor relations program. If management does understand the true purpose, correct decisions about ethical considerations will follow naturally.

The purpose of an investor relations program should be to provide a continuous flow of all pertinent information about the securities of

JOHN F. CHILDS is Vice President, Irving Trust Company, New York, New York.

the company, both good and bad, on an equal basis to all persons who may have an interest in it. Once a company goes public, the only way a stockholder can get his money back is through the sale of the stock in the market. Stockholders have a right to be able to buy and sell the stock of a company at a price that is openly arrived at through the processes of the securities market. It is only through a policy of complete disclosure that the price will be determined in this manner. Sometimes it seems easy and natural for managements to come to consider their role in investor relations as being salesmen. Actually, their function is not to sell or interpret but to make available the information on which opinions can be formed.

Unfortunately, a company can get off on the wrong foot in an investor relations program. A company usually initiates such a program when its operations are successful. This leads to widespread interest in the company; and as a result, company representatives are often invited to appear before an analysts' society to tell their story, and they make a "sales pitch," perhaps in glowing terms, on the past performance and future prospects of the company. Then if the company has a bad year, management may be at a loss as to what to do because it did not realize in the first place that sound investor relations involves disclosing both the good and the bad news. More likely than not, management will clam up in such a situation and cancel meetings before the analysts. As a matter of fact, one can often tell when there is a slump in business conditions by the number of such cancellations.

A company is off on the wrong track if it lets the price of its stock be the barometer of its investor relations activities. When stock prices are high, management may be afraid to talk because of the danger of pushing them still higher; or when the stock goes way down, management may feel that it should do more with the investor relations program. The price of stock may indicate that the company has been issuing information that is too bullish or too bearish, but this should in no way affect the principle of continually giving out all the information all the time.

Still further on this point, some companies feel that their managers should not appear before groups of analysts unless they have some startling news to tell, and they therefore postpone these appearances far too long. They fail to realize that the analysts will become better informed by a regular flow of information rather than by the infrequent release of spectacular news.

The question of ethical considerations arises again in connection with the type of information that is given out to both insiders and to outsiders. A glance at some annual reports tells us clearly that the management team has no basic conception of what is to be accomplished. Some glamorized, "public relations" types of annual reports fail to give the complete story of what happened to the company during the year and why. Some reports, whether this is intentional or not, are masterpieces of evasion. Very often even the footnotes reveal a company's lack of understanding; they do not provide enough information to be of any value to analysts.

Excuses sometimes given for failing to report adequate financial information are as follows: "It is impossible to supply all the information the financial analysts want." "It is hard to tell what they want." "We will have to wait until the picture clarifies before we can explain the problem." These are poor excuses. Securities are bought and sold every day: stock transactions don't wait for problems to be solved. The financial officer of any company of reasonable size should have sufficient contact with financial experts to know what they want. Another excuse that management may use to avoid giving out information is that it may reveal "inside" facts to the competition and that this would be detrimental to stockholders. Analysts must accept this if it is true, but in many instances analysts are able to get the information from the competition.

Where new issues are concerned, the Securities Act requires full disclosure, and there are severe penalties for failing to do so. From the point of view of investors, the idea of full disclosure is just as essential as regards outstanding securities. There seems to be some justification for having the same restrictions apply to material in annual reports and similar documents as to that which goes into a prospectus.

Then there is the problem of the insider who profits from his knowledge. The Securities Act covers situations where an insider makes a profit from the purchase and sale of stock within a six-month period: such profits must be turned over to the company. There is no reason, ethically speaking, why the same rule should not apply beyond the six-month period. Some situations might arise like the one in which the officers and directors of a company know that shortly a favorable announcement will be made which should push up the price of a stock, and they purchase stock for themselves or their wives. There is no way to justify such action no matter how long stock is owned.

There are numerous other people who may get inside information and misuse it. A director may be a partner in a brokerage firm and use his inside information to keep the financial analyst in his firm better informed. This is obviously wrong, and a company must be meticulous in making sure that such a director in no way uses information to his own benefit or to that of his firm.

An investment banker or a commercial banker may require information such as a forecast of earnings in order to be able to advise the company properly on financing. However, management must guard against the use of such material for the personal advantage of financial experts or that of their companies.

Some companies are known and respected for the meticulous attention they pay to prevent any leaks on earnings, dividend policy, financing, and so on. They see to it that everyone gets important financial news at the same time. Old-timers on Wall Street disregard completely anyone who says he has some inside information about such companies. We might wish that some others would have equally rigid standards.

In the cultivation of the financial community, no preference should be shown any one analyst or group of analysts. In a small meeting with a select group of security analysts the following comment was made by the management of the host company: "You are a select group of experienced security analysts. We want to bring you up to date, but we wish to be confidential and not broadcast our comments all over the financial community; that is why we kept the group small." This is a dangerous approach. It is sometimes necessary in an investor relations program to have luncheons with small groups and trips over a company's properties which are limited to a relatively few analysts. The financial community understands this, and a company should not shy away from working with small groups; but it should do so only if it fits into a general plan for keeping the financial community better informed. It should always be careful to guard against any sign of favoritism.

Part of the problem of favoritism involves answering questions of analysts. If a bright analyst asks some good questions about a company's operations and the company provides the answers, should it feel duty bound to give the answers to all analysts? Certainly not, if the answers are within the range of that material which the company will give all analysts if it is asked. Such information as forecasts of earnings and dividends would obviously not fall in this category. Those in charge of investor relations should pay attention to the searching questions analysts ask because these questions provide a guide to the type of material the company should use in its future program.

It goes without saying that lavish entertainment or gifts of significant value have no place in an investor relations program. However, a company should not be prudish about buying meals, paying the hotel bills, and so forth where these are justifiable and pertinent to the company's relationships. Many companies invite groups of analysts to visit their plants. Usually, both the analysts and the company officials feel it is proper for the company to pay their transportation.

At times, a company may embark on a program to purchase its own stock to be used in acquisition of other companies. Such stock purchases are generally handled through a brokerage house. The company should set up a detailed procedure to prevent the possibility of anyone on the inside being accused of taking advantage of the situation. This includes eliminating all officers and directors from making any purchases or sales during the period when the company is acquiring stock and setting up a strict procedure as to how the brokerage house should act.

If a company hires an outside firm to handle its investor relations, it may have some nice questions to answer. Can an outsider, who is in a position between the company and the investor, properly tell the story? Will such a firm be willing to tell the bad news as well as the good? Part of the job of security analysts involves appraisal of management. Does the use of a third party prevent the analysts from having an opportunity to appraise management? In other words, if a company does use an outside firm, it will face a new set of ethical considerations, such as whether the outside firm's compensation for service should include stock or stock options. This method is obviously in conflict with the true purpose of investor relations.

A sound investor relations program will benefit a company and its stockholders for many reasons. Aside from these benefits, however, management must realize its obligations to carry out such a program. Properly conceived, it is in no way a glamorous part of management's job. Those who have observed the companies which do a good job know that they handle their investor relations in an atmosphere of the highest dignity and with the soundest ethical standards.

# ECONOMIC EDUCATION FOR INVESTORS •

RUDDICK C. LAWRENCE

IT HAS BEEN SAID THAT THE most disappointed people in the world are those who get what's coming to them. Whether or not you agree with that wry generalization, it must be admitted that most people are rather adept at finding others to blame for their own disappointments.

The realistic businessman, however, knows that spilled milk is seldom marketable, and his time is more wisely spent in developing better containers and teaching people how to use them. But in the area of investor relations—and investor education in particular—some otherwise perceptive businessmen have avoided making mistakes simply by not doing anything at all.

Individual executives, of course, have long recognized the importance of the share owner in the overall corporate structure; and many have done an impressive job of keeping share owners—and prospective investors—accurately informed about their companies' activities. Only recently, however, has the business community begun to recognize the magnitude of its stake in the general economic education of investors.

By and large, American management has reacted to this discovery with vigor and imagination. Much has been accomplished. Yet, much more remains to be done if 17 million investors are to function as an informed economic electorate and play an articulate role in the nation's economic affairs. The validity of this goal is underscored by the plain statistical fact that the nation's share owner population today equals or outnumbers the membership of trade unions. But certainly no one would suggest that

RUDDICK C. LAWRENCE is Vice President, New York Stock Exchange, New York, New York.

share owners' views are presented to the nation's economic policy makers as effectively as the views of organized labor.

The business community can help remedy this situation by strengthening its efforts in the field of economic education. Many large corporations, for example, assign responsibility for share owner relations to high-ranking members of the management team. Too often, however, these executives concern themselves almost exclusively with describing and interpreting the company's performance. This is certainly an important part of their job. But a broader view of their responsibilities would encompass the need to keep share owners informed about economic developments beyond the realm of the company's own activities—and to encourage the individual share owner to take an active interest in national economic affairs.

The American share owner is probably better informed than his counterparts the world over; but he is still, in economic matters, woefully undereducated. The dramatic growth in share ownership during the single decade 1952-1962—from 6.5 million to 17 million individuals—underscores the increasing prominence of the investor in the business community. Clearly, the needs and wishes of these millions of individuals—and their knowledgeability—will be crucial factors in determining this country's business climate in the years ahead.

Where should the necessary educational effort begin? Logically, the foundations should be shaped in the nation's schools and colleges. It is no secret that in the past many educational institutions treated economics as a luxury rather than as an important element of basic curriculum. Improvement of this situation is necessary, and it is gratifying that in recent years educators have begun to pay increasing attention to economics as a subject for general study.

The Joint Council on Economic Education is presently conducting a survey of economics courses offered to students in the public school systems of 130 American cities with populations of over 100,000. The 98 school systems which have reported to date account for approximately one-fourth of the nation's total public school enrollment. A majority of the reporting school systems have done curriculum-revision work in social studies or business education during the past three years. Economics is now a required course in 25 of these systems and is offered as an elective in 66 others; only 7 of the 98 offer no economics courses at all. And while comparable statistics have not been compiled for colleges and universities, it is safe to say that there is scarcely a major institution in the country today which does not offer at least introductory courses in economics.

All of this is encouraging and bodes well for the future—as does the business community's increasing effort to aid schools in their search for ideas and materials to facilitate the teaching of practical economics. The New York Stock Exchange has pioneered a "Stock Gifts To Minors" program, through which adults can readily introduce youngsters to the investment process and encourage them, through personal ownership of stocks, to develop an early interest in economics. Today, nearly half a million young people own shares in America's corporations, and all 50 states have passed legislation to simplify this particular gift-giving process.

But what about today's adult investors—and the vast majority of some 35 million potential share owners who are past school age? This is where the entire business community can do an important job. The Exchange's 1962 Census of Shareowners revealed that better than 4 out of 5 adult share owners are high school graduates, more than half have some college training, and nearly one-third are college graduates. These proportions are all substantially higher than the national averages for all adults.

In view of these facts, a report of the Public Opinion Index for Industry published in late 1961 by Opinion Research Corporation, "Word Barriers in Stockholder Communications," documents a degree of economic illiteracy among share owners which is particularly shocking and challenging. This survey showed that "most stockholders are poorly equipped to handle many widely used financial terms" which appear in annual reports. Nearly half the stockholders interviewed said they got "little or nothing" from formal financial statements. A majority of them were unable to define such terms as "assets," "earnings," "inflation," "depreciation," or "depletion allowances"—despite the researchers' willingness to accept almost any definition which indicated some familiarity with the concept involved.

These distressing revelations supplemented and confirmed the findings of an earlier study conducted among share owners and prospective share owners by the Exchange. As part of a survey of public attitudes toward investing, the Exchange had asked some 3,000 share owners and non-share owners: "Would you like to know more about common stock?" and "What information would you like?"

The responses to these questions have helped shape the subsequent course of the Exchange's informational and educational programs. We learned, for example, that among non-share owners who were thinking seriously about investing, 61 per cent felt a need for more information—as did 52 per cent of those who already owned stock. Among the types of information most frequently cited were: "basic information on what stock is all about," "how stocks are bought and sold," "how stock exchanges work," "how to read stock market tables," "how to evaluate a company," and "how to read a balance sheet."

Traditionally, the Exchange has placed considerable emphasis on listed companies' obligations to their share owners in such matters as timely disclosure of corporate developments which may affect stock values, solicitation of proxies, and periodic reporting of financial data. And we have gone on record supporting legislation now before Congress which would extend many of these requirements to major publicly held companies which are not listed on a stock exchange.

At the same time, we have recognized that it can be an empty gesture to give share owners this information if they are unable to understand what you are talking about. We have long believed that no one should invest—not even those who are financially able to take the necessary risks—unless he or she has at least a general knowledge of how the free enterprise system works and how corporations are structured and operate. And as part of our overall effort to encourage broader share ownership on a sound basis, we have undertaken an extensive range of informational and educational activities embracing virtually every aspect of the economics of investing.

For example, we publish some 8 million pieces of literature annually—on subjects ranging from "The Language of Investing" and "Careers in Stocks and Bonds" to the Exchange community's views on securities industry regulation and tax questions of particular interest to investors. Materials which may be suitable for distribution by listed companies and other business organizations are made available to them at cost. Our national advertising program—budgeted at about $1 million annually—stresses "the right versus the wrong way to invest," the services offered by Exchange member brokers, and the Exchange community's systems of self-regulation.

The Exchange is the producer of numerous films and radio and television programs on investing; the publisher of a monthly magazine for investors; the operator of a unique exhibit hall and visitors' gallery visited by more than a half million people each year; and a tireless aide to all news media—including company publications—which are eager to provide their readers and listeners with timely information about investing.

Many Exchange member organizations maintain their own public relations and educational programs. These firms often supplement their own activities and publications with materials prepared by the Exchange; and they frequently gear their local advertising programs to tie in with the Exchange's national ad campaigns.

Some 3,000 member-firm brokers are active participants in Investors' Information Committees—the heart of the Exchange community's cooperative educational program—in nearly 100 leading cities across the country. These committees maintain active speakers' bureaus to fill speaking engagements, conduct lecture courses on investing, and participate in a series of public forums in conjunction with leading newspapers. In 1962 alone, member-organization brokers, using materials prepared by the Exchange, delivered an estimated 50,000 lectures before audiences totaling more than one million people—at evening schools for adults, community and business centers, and on radio and television. Exchange publications and educational materials are distributed through the Investors' Information Program to schools and colleges throughout the country, where they are frequently incorporated into the standard teaching curricula.

The Stock Exchange, of course, is in a unique position to perform these public educational services. However, there are many investors whom we cannot reach directly—for example, those individual share owners who may not *actively* seek information or who may not know how to go about acquiring it. For while the Exchange does know that these people exist in large numbers, we do not know their names and addresses. But the companies in which they own shares *do* know who they are and can keep in touch with them. These companies have both the opportunity and the ability to provide their share owners with educational materials which are attractive as well as informative. By relating general economic issues to their own companies' activities, they can demonstrate that share owners have a practical self-interest—perhaps the strongest incentive to learning—in acquiring a better understanding of these issues. In recent years, more and more corporations—and not only the largest ones—have recognized that there is a job they can do in this area; and it is vastly encouraging to see them accepting the challenge.

Realizing that many corporations are seeking help in this undertaking, the Exchange has developed a program to assist its listed companies in improving their communications with share owners, employees, the financial community, and the general public. We have served as a clearinghouse for informational techniques which have been developed and used successfully by these companies. And, in this capacity, we have been able to observe the steady and often dramatic improvement in the quantity, quality, and range of informational materials prepared and distributed by companies to their share owners. Indeed, to keep pace with company activities in this field, the Exchange plans to speed up its own service to listed companies by publishing special bulletins on subjects of particular interest to officials in charge of company communications.

As recently as ten years ago, an interested observer would have been hard pressed to discover many outstanding examples of annual reports, company magazines, or special publications which paid more than casual attention to the individual share owner's need for economic information presented in understandable language. The typical annual report, for example, seemed to be written by financial experts, primarily for the edification of other financial experts. The typical company magazine was chockful of statistics on the activities of the company bowling league.

To be sure, many companies still cling to these practices—and their managements are probably wondering why they aren't receiving the degree of investor interest to which they feel entitled. They are among those disappointed people who get what's coming to them!

But contrast the ordinary facts-and-figures annual report with the following excerpts from the 1962 report to share owners by George Olmsted, Jr., president of the S. D. Warren Company. Under the heading, "Depreciation and 'Cash Flow'—and What They Do for a Business," there is a brief description of the effect of the Internal Revenue Service's new depreciation guidelines and the new 7 per cent business investment credit. Then, the report continues:

> If the foregoing sounds like "accounting gobbledygook" to you, I'm not surprised.
>
> Few people, it seems to me—and this is particularly true of the "average investor"—*really* understand depreciation and cash flow.
>
> And yet the new depreciation rates, coupled with the 7 per cent credit, have an important bearing on the future welfare and strength of many companies. And so if you are to evaluate a company properly—whether you are a security analyst or a shareholder or an investor—if you are to evaluate a company properly and compare it with others, you *must* understand cash flow. And as time goes on it is my belief that folks will more and more look to cash flow in a company as one of *the most vital* measuring sticks in evaluating and comparing one industry with another—one company with another.
>
> So what follows is a bit of a crusade, if you will—an attempt at a simplified version of Economics 1-2.

And what follows is, indeed, an astonishingly clear explanation of how the company interprets an often misused term, "cash flow," which, according to the Opinion Research Corporation survey, is understood by only one out of every 20 stockholders.

Later in the same report, the reader encounters the following:

> Any of you shareholders who happens to be in the vicinity of Portland, Maine, or Muskegon, Michigan, should drop in to visit *your* property. You will be most welcome. If you're in Maine, ask for Rudy Greep. If you're in Michigan, ask for Frank Roberts. They are both Vice Presidents—and each is the responsible head for his particular mill.

> You will see logs of wood going in one end of the plant and finished paper coming out the other. It's a fascinating process. You'll enjoy the visit. And we'll enjoy having you.

Granted that the corporation with hundreds of thousands of share owners might find the folksy approach inappropriate, there are hundreds of smaller publicly held companies in this country which could effectively develop their own variations.

And there is no reason why even the corporate giant should consider itself above explaining its economic views and interpreting the mysteries of financial terminology—as well as terms and business concepts which may be peculiar to its own industry—to its share owners. In fact, the larger the company, the greater its obligation to a wider circle of individual investors.

The most widely held company of all, American Telephone and Telegraph, welcomes each new share owner with an attractive booklet explaining the company's business philosophy and describing its activities. On a somewhat smaller scale, but nonetheless effectively, such companies as Miles Laboratories and Falstaff Brewing acquaint new share owners with the scope of their activities.

Some companies have issued special educational publications focusing on specific economic concepts. Over the years, DuPont has produced and distributed an excellent series of informational booklets; a recent addition to this series, *The Profit Motive,* begins with this striking headline: "PROFIT: Whatever you call it, however you count it, profit is basic and indispensable to all societies, including Crusoe's and Khrushchev's." It goes on to present a 32-page explanation of profits, in terms and with illustrations and examples which most share owners can readily relate to their own experience. Under the title *This We Believe . . .*, Pennsylvania Bell distributed a handy 16-page booklet reprinting a series of advertisements through which the company "sought to make the social and economic essentiality of profits clear."

Other companies have made special efforts to alert their share owners to legislative matters affecting their interests. General Electric and American Telephone and Telegraph have used the medium of the annual report to present management's views on tax policy. Bristol-Myers, St. Regis Paper, and Babcock and Wilcox all notified their share owners of the companies' reasons for opposing measures which would increase double taxation of dividend income.

Increasingly, the company magazine has become an important vehicle for explaining many complex aspects of economic affairs to employees, many of whom are also investors in other companies. Particularly noteworthy among scores of excellent articles which have appeared in employee publications are New York Bell's word-and-picture study of the tax-making powers of the House Ways and Means Committee; Pfizer's illustrated feature on the European Common Market; Sunray's special study—subsequently reprinted and given additional distribution—of the cost-price squeeze; National Gypsum's informative feature on the "invention" of the corporation; Warner-Lambert's question-and-answer explanation of stock ownership; Minnesota Mining's description of how the financial community channels job-creating capital into American industry.

Outstanding in their respective media are American Can Company's widely distributed study of the growth of this country's economic system, *The American Achievement,* which initially appeared as a complete 22-page issue of the company's employee magazine, and Scott Paper Company's special student edition of its annual report, clearly annotated to explain the significance of each item in the report and defining terms with which student readers may not be acquainted.

Obviously, no one can deny that the American business community has made impressive progress in the vital campaign to eliminate economic illiteracy in this country. But no one can deny that a great deal remains to be done. The job is one which must be shared by educational institutions, the securities industry, and business management.

The range of potential activities which companies can adapt to their own particular situations is almost limitless. Special educational events can be programed for annual meetings, and supplementary literature can be provided through meeting announcements and postmeeting reports. Advertising can be used for educational as well as sales messages to reach broad public audiences. Plant tours have been used successfully by many companies to acquaint share owners with production and research activities and to build public understanding and goodwill. Employee education need not be limited to company publications, as a number of imaginative internal programs—classes in economics, reading racks and libraries, company forums—have demonstrated to individual organizations which have been willing to pioneer in these areas.

Admittedly, it is not a simple matter to translate into clear and readily understandable terms the details of the complex economic structure upon which our free enterprise system is based. Nor is it easy to popularize the interplay of incentives, profits, competition, productive capacity, and literally scores of similarly "difficult" concepts which are part of the businessman's everyday vocabulary.

Yet future economic growth will depend in large measure on the success with which we tackle this formidable challenge. The free enterprise system cannot flourish and expand without the active participation of millions of individual Americans who are able to invest part of their personal savings in new and growing enterprises.

But if these people are to decide for themselves whether to take the necessary risks, then we must see to it that they not only understand the activities and goals of particular companies in which they may be interested but also recognize the relationship of those companies to the overall economic system. In addition, and perhaps most important of all, we must encourage them to accept their own responsibilities as share owners, as employees, and as citizens to take an active and meaningful role in economic affairs.

The New York Stock Exchange has estimated that the nation's share owner population may reach 25 million by 1970. This is an exciting prospect. Clearly, it offers every forward-looking management group special opportunities to attract fresh capital and wide support and understanding. The extent to which each company develops those opportunities will help determine the extent to which it—and the entire business community—will share in America's economic growth. Those who react vigorously and imaginatively to the challenge will get what's coming to them—and they won't be disappointed.

# BROADENING SHARE OWNERSHIP •

**O. GLENN SAXON, Jr.**

WILL MOST COMPANIES, 40 YEARS FROM NOW, be financed by share owners who have voluntarily saved in order to be able to become capitalists and earn money on their money, or will new business expansion programs involve some type of forced savings and directed investment administered by the government or some other agency? The things that investor-owned companies do now to further broaden share ownership will to a great extent determine the answer to this question.

If we look ahead, say four decades, we can postulate that at the rate of increase of the past 50 years there should then be at least eight to ten times as much energy available for each person in our society and for each productive worker. The world is becoming a single, competitive market—characterized by kaleidoscopic changes in science, technology, and engineering and in their applications to the needs of man. The sharper, swifter pace of competition will see the process of change itself become the norm: the birth of whole new products, the creation of new industries—familiar enough phenomena today—will become even more typical of the business scene. So, too, will the death of the old and the obsolete.

For the individual, such changes present great opportunities, but hazards and uncertainties as well—for some, the loss of a job; for many more, the need to acquire periodically new skills or revamped training. With such changes, significant income instability can occur. One answer to these changes is for each individual to receive relatively more of his income through investment. If share ownership can be broadened both in numbers of people and in the average amount of individual holdings, we may well see the day when, for millions of families, income from invested capital may rival in importance income from labor. Thereby, investment could become a significant force for promoting economic security for

O. GLENN SAXON, JR. is Consultant—Professional Investor Relations, General Electric Company, New York, New York.

many Americans. Those on retirement incomes could also enjoy an increased independence and dignity through greater ownership of stock.

## THE CHALLENGE IN PERSPECTIVE

Our competitive business system is at a crucial stage in its struggle for needed support and understanding from its owners and the general public. The next few years may be the time of decision as to whether our nation will grow into an ever more broadly based free enterprise economy. It is the role of investor relations to develop needed support for and understanding of business by encouraging broad share ownership and better economic and investment education.

History suggests that wherever a civilization has shown real durability and vitality, it has been because the individual citizens somehow were infused with a sense of personal involvement in the survival and growth of the community. For whatever variety of motives, the individual felt a personal responsibility to play a role in maintaining the strength and progress of his system. This was true in the years of the ascendancy of Greece and Rome and—through the emergence of an active property-owning middle class—in the rise of our own economic and political system.

One of the strong underlying forces making for such a sense of responsibility and personal involvement is the widely available opportunity for all in our economy to become owners—owners of private property in whatever form it may take. Home ownership, for example, promotes a sense of the citizen's responsibility for the community in which he lives. More to the point, however, is the ownership of shares in broadly held corporations. This is one of the most significant forms of private ownership, because of its implications for the citizen's sense of a personal stake in the performance of the economic system. And a measure of the triumph of this economic system is that, with the corporate form of ownership, everyone can actually share in owning, providing capital for, and profiting from the creative economic force of our era, the corporation.

In order to build this potential into the actuality of a more effective free competitive system for the future, business must take positive action to encourage and stimulate individuals to participate much more fully and directly in the risks and rewards of ownership of business. Only a broadly based capitalism will attract supporters of the free enterprise system in numbers sufficient to sustain it.

Perhaps one of the reasons for the century-old appeal of socialism, especially in other lands, has been its deceptive promise of what it calls "public ownership." Everybody owns everything; yet no one owns anything. The promise proves hollow precisely because the socialists so-called public ownership brings no real sense of individual responsibility and involvement. Quite the contrary, it holds out to the individual the enervating notion that things will be taken care of *for* him.

### THE OPPORTUNITIES OF BROADER SHARE OWNERSHIP

A share in the ownership of America's great business enterprises, large and small, on the other hand, throws the individual squarely into the middle of economic processes. He finds himself making judgments about the business prospects of this or that company, and he finds that he has a serious stake in arriving at sound decisions affecting his own well-being and that of those dependent on him.

As more people become direct owners, the companies involved will communicate with them about the joint interests of the companies and the owners. This, by the way, is a further opportunity for the companies to develop support for the system of private ownership. But they must first recognize the crying need for the development of more constructive relationships between companies and their owners. The job they have to do today is one of preventive anticipation. The Berle and Means thesis of the divorce of ownership from responsibility has widespread currency today. We are all cognizant of the Security and Exchange Commission's voluminous study of the securities markets and peripheral activities. We have seen the rise of the so-called professional share owner who has become in so many instances a mere raucous heckler. These are but symptoms of an underlying restlessness and problem. If companies do not actively try to develop more effective ways of getting share owners to participate more fully in a constructive role, they may face a time when the politicians of a future era will seek new levels or modes of regulation for publicly held corporations in the guise of protecting the share owners and the public interest. Insofar as business is able to encourage owners to become and act like direct share owners and actively to follow the affairs of and participate in their companies, this threat will vanish.

In addition to such long-range advantages, many companies will benefit more directly from the growth and success of the special plans that have been adopted in recent years to encourage broader employee share ownership. Certainly it is unlikely that mere ownership of stock in the company he works for is going to make a union member change sides in a labor dispute; but as his stake in ownership of the enterprise increases, this ownership will create major opportunities for the company.

The growing worth of an employee's stake in the company will increasingly facilitate communicating with him regularly. As ownership becomes more important as an economic factor in his life, his own interest in the facts of business life as they apply to his company will grow. Ownership makes it easier to tell the story of profits and their benefits and how hard they are to achieve. It helps reveal the employee's and the company's common interests. It can serve to make more real and understandable the many ways in which all in our economy benefit from business success: as employees, as part owners of the business, and as customers. And it can develop in an employee a new sense of identification with the company when he receives annual and quarterly reports, attends annual meetings, and learns more of what his capital at work means and accomplishes.

The impact of all this—providing that the company fully utilizes its new opportunities to communicate with employees—may be to encourage the employee to recognize himself for what he in fact is and has been all along—a multiple participant in our economy. His well-being does not depend solely upon his role as wage earner or union member, but also upon his role as customer (price levels, inflation, availability of the goods he desires as a result of the smooth functioning of the market); his role as an owner (directly in his own company and perhaps in other companies, but also indirectly through his pension plan, his savings account, his life insurance, and perhaps through other means); his role as a citizen, because he periodically votes on public matters which directly or indirectly affect his well-being and success in each of his other roles. The company must ask itself if it can successfully communicate the importance of these roles to each owner in a balanced manner so that he will understand, act, vote, and work for himself in what he recognizes to be his own best interest.

### THE RISE IN SHARE OWNERSHIP

Since 1952, there has been an explosive growth in the number of persons who are direct share owners. In that year, the Brookings Institute reported some 6.5 million Americans owned stock. By 1962, according to a recent New York Stock Exchange survey, more than 17 million people—one adult in every six—owned shares of stock in American business.

But if we look at the people in our economy who still do not own stock, we find that we have barely scratched the surface of potential ownership. More than 50 million people own Government savings bonds; over 130 million own life insurance; and more than 85 million have savings accounts. If we look at people in terms of their income levels, we find that over 50 per cent of households with incomes in excess of $25,000 a year still do not own stock—and more than 60 per cent of those earning $15,000 to $25,000 per year are not owners. Even in the highest income brackets, there is a substantial proportion of potential investors who own no stock whatsoever.

Of the greatest significance in creating a meaningful broadening of share ownership in recent years have been two developments: first, the rapid growth of company-sponsored plans for encouraging employee share ownership and, second, the spectacular growth of mutual funds.

Employee stock-purchase plans take many forms; and while in most cases they do not push out large amounts of stock to each employee each year, they have the virtue of steady accumulation. Over the years, the individual employee in many plans can develop a fairly substantial holding of stock in his company as compared with his other assets. And from this experience with stock ownership in one company often comes an interest in investing in other companies.

By dint of aggressive salesmanship, the number of share owners of investment companies (mutual funds and others) has more than tripled since 1954 to 5.9 million. Again, the growth of mutual funds seems to have encouraged broader direct ownership of shares over a period of time, for many who originally invested through a fund have later come into the market as direct investors.

In recent years, another development, fascinating as far as its effectiveness in economic and investment education but of not as great significance in terms of dollars, has been the investment club movement. The investment clubs that have sprung up all over the country are a most effective technique for do-it-yourself teaching of investors at minimum personal risk, and they have contributed much to the broadening of share ownership.

For many years, and especially for the 20 years following 1929, most people embarked on adult life without having any exposure to the investment process either at school or in the home, and the very name of Wall Street was anathema. As a result, share ownership is still surrounded with the mystique of the unknown. Proper educational efforts should do much to overcome such apprehensions, but what little is now being done seems inadequate to meet the interest already aroused. The investment club movement "just grew" as a way of helping to meet this need.

In the typical investment club, some 10 to 25 persons get together and contribute as little as $5 or $10 each per month which is then invested after investigation and discussion by the club. The objective is to learn how better to invest money, and this is done in a way that minimizes the risk of any individual member. Emphasis is placed on studying the investment process, in carefully investigating investment opportunities, and in then selecting a given company based upon careful evaluation. By this self-help educational process, a substantial number of adequately informed, investment-oriented individuals are introduced to the market in a constructive and reasonable way, although very few expert investors are developed.

To help service the increasing number of share owners and to promote broader ownership among all individuals, the financial community is constantly improving and expanding its facilities. Registered representatives of the New York Stock Exchange brokerage firms alone have almost tripled since 1950 and now number over 32,000. The branch offices of these firms have doubled since 1950 and now number over 3,400. The monthly investment plans—first available in 1954—now number more than 100,000.

Obviously the mass of share owners today are new investors with only ten years of experience in the stock market. They may have been attracted by rising stock prices, but the approach they are taking to investing suggests otherwise. Most of these new investors seem to be taking a long-term savings approach through company plans, monthly investment plans, or mutual funds.

To fulfill the expectations of these millions of new investors, business will have to grow more profitable in the future. But, to discharge its obligation to these people completely, it will have to do more than be profitable. It will have to explain profits and the free enterprise system to gain their active support and understanding. It will have to help share owners to protect their investments and their own interests from restrictions which might further limit profit potentials.

Share owners already have one ear tuned in to business leaders; therefore, they can be mobilized to help build a better business climate. In reality, share owners expect their employees—the managers to whom they have entrusted the business—to speak out about issues that affect their companies. Inertia alone stands in the way, and it can and must be overcome.

Business alone cannot be expected to carry the full burden of economic education. Stock exchanges, mutual funds, brokerage firms, insurance companies, banks, financial intermediaries, and others—all have a natural stake in the vast educational program that must be undertaken. Certainly insurance companies, commercial and savings banks, and pension funds have a special responsibility to explain the ravages of inflation, especially to those it hurts the most—the elderly. Stock exchanges, mutual funds, brokerage firms, and investment bankers have the critical problem of gaining more understanding of the importance of private capital formation to the free enterprise system. All those in the financial community as well as in business should pull together in the task of spreading an understanding of the fundamentals: profits, reinvestment of earnings, taxes, and so on.

These educational programs will not only result in a more informed share owner body but be important stimulants to broadening individual stock ownership. If we do not explain the free enterprise system and if new methods of acquiring stock are not developed and aggressively promoted, the trend toward more institutional ownership will far outdistance and far outweigh individual ownership in its implications.

There are, of course, many beneficial effects flowing from some of these ways of enabling individuals to participate in ownership through institutional holdings. However, the advantage of personal involvement and risk which flows from direct individual ownership may be seriously weakened by too strong a future trend toward increased institutional ownership. However beneficial it may be as one of several forces in the securities markets, institutional ownership may eventually reduce direct individual ownership to a minimum.

Since 1900, the share of financial intermediaries (or investment institutions) in the wealth and in the income flows of our economy has been steadily increasing. Between 1900 and 1952, according to a study by Raymond W. Goldsmith for the National Bureau of Economic Research in 1958, the following happened:

1. The share of financial intermediaries in ownership of domestic stock outstanding rose from 7.6 per cent ($12.3 billion) to 20.5 per cent ($195 billion).
2. Private pension fund assets rose from nothing to $9 billion.
3. Personal trust department funds increased from $3 billion to $6 billion.

Between 1949 and 1963, according to the New York Stock Exchange, the market value of holdings by certain institutions (not including personal trust, but adding in nonprofit institutions) of listed stocks rose from 12.7 per cent of the outstanding market value in 1949 to 18.9 per cent in 1962. Noninsured pension funds increased their ownership of listed stock from $.5 billion to $17.2 billion; open-end investment companies rose from $1.4 billion to $15.6 billion.

The rapid rate of increase since 1949 is likely to continue. This trend may also be influenced by increased stock ownership by mutual savings banks and the probability that life insurance companies will continue to move more aggressively in the selling of plans such as variable annuity contracts.

Thus we see two opposing trends at work currently. The stronger one at the present time seems to be the push toward increasing the relative size of large, institutional holdings. If this movement should continue unabated, the time will come when institutional ownership, good though it is in moderation, may so dominate the market that it would begin to act as a depressant on individual direct ownership.

### A NEW LOOK AT THE OPPORTUNITIES

If we are to achieve our goal of broader individual share ownership, we must now begin to encourage new thinking and experimentation to this end. The potential for creative solutions in this area is immense. The amount of serious study that has been given to this problem seems rather slight. More attention has been paid in recent years to the roadblocks than to development of ways around them. These roadblocks are real, but they may not be insurmountable if there is enough economic incentive to make the creation of a solution worthwhile.

For example, the common complaint of brokers that it costs too much to service small accounts and that therefore they desire only large customers cannot be cavalierly dismissed. On the other hand, is it not possible to develop procedures for handling brokerage paperwork which could sharply reduce these costs? Something of this sort must be done before any satisfactory broad sales effort is likely to be mounted by brokers or expected to carry its full weight. What can be done to ease the problems of paperwork that surround stock transfers? Is it completely impossible to issue stock certificates in a form which can be handled satisfactorily by modern data-processing equipment?

A real need of the novice investor is for adequate investment advice. What techniques can be developed to help speed the flow of accurate information and higher-quality analytical reports economically and profitably to smaller investors? How can top-quality investment analyses be geared to the knowledge level of the beginning investor?

There have been proposals to encourage companies to split their shares on a regular basis so as to keep the market price around the $10 to $20 level as a way of encouraging potential buyers to invest earlier. Could this kind of proposal be carried out at a reasonable cost, and would it really constitute a step toward the goal?

Are there ways a broker could help a beginning investor to achieve a balanced, through small, portfolio early in his investment experience? Could a special odd-lot commission be developed which would enable a new investor to buy, say, one share in each of ten companies at a commission charge similar to what would be charged if the ten shares were all in one company?

What more can companies, brokerage firms, and others do to encourage and promote the responsible investment clubs?

Are there ways in which the fast-growing area of pension plans could be progressively somewhat de-institutionalized? Is it possible to develop some options whereby an individual pension plan member can choose, from among several program alternatives, the investment policy for his particular share of the fund which would best reflect his individual wealth, his future needs, and his expectations? Can various options be made available at retirement so a pensioner can choose, if he so desires, to take an investment portfolio rather than his monthly pension payments?

### BROADER EFFORTS NEEDED

Besides encouraging new thinking about the problems which are slowing the growth of individual share ownership, individuals and companies can directly contribute by participating in or developing programs which will:

1. Promote economic and investment education.
2. Communicate more fully to owners and seek their help and understanding more actively, as a means of getting fuller participation and support.
3. Encourage share owners to become active supporters of our business system—by sponsoring economic and investor education programs, by writing their elected representatives to express their points of view, and by asking all the companies they own to become active proponents of broader ownership.
4. Develop better employee share ownership plans.
5. Foster more communication by institutional investors to beneficial owners of the economic and investment facts of life.
6. Establish planned programs of economic education for share owners in every company.
7. Support organizations active in investment or economic education.

In the broadest sense, economics and politics—the ways people earn their livings and govern themselves—are so closely related they must be considered as one. Key events, changes in underlying patterns, or fundamental conceptual changes in the one area necessarily affect the other.

There have been two major trends in the share ownership of American business since 1900: one toward larger numbers of direct share owners and another toward increased holdings of stock by institutions. To build a sound ownership structure for business over the years, the trend toward institutionalization must be balanced by the growth of direct individual ownership. Business must take positive action to encourage and stimulate individuals to participate much more broadly and directly in the risks and the rewards of ownership of business. Finally, there is a need for the development and support of specific programs which can contribute toward more direct ownership of business by more people and which will at the same time effectively help to open their eyes to the greater opportunities they have as multiple participants—employees, customers, owners, all at the same time—in a free business system.

# INDEX

# INDEX

C



D



E



F

G



I



J

L



M



N



O



P

## R



## S

U



V



W